Tasmania

Belongs to:

ᴇᴅᴡᴀʀᴅ & ᴛʜᴇʀᴇѕᴀ ᴄᴏᴏᴘᴇʀ

Please return when read, thanks.

Tasmania

Little Hills Press .

Little Hills Press, 2000
© Maps prepared by Mapgraphics Pty Ltd.
© Photographs, Department of Tourism, Tasmania, and Little Hills Press

Cover by Artitude
Printed in Singapore
© Michael Cook 2000
Revised and updated

ISBN 1 86315 141 9

Little Hills Press
37-43 Alexander Street, Crows Nest NSW 2065 Australia

Disclaimer
Whilst all care has been taken by the publisher and author to ensure that the
information is accurate and up to date, the publisher does not take responsibility
for the information published herein. The recommendations are those of the
author, and as things get better or worse, places close down and others open,
some elements in the book may be inaccurate when you get there. Please write
and tell us about it so we can update the text in subsequent editions.

Little Hills and are registered trademarks of Little Hills Press Pty Ltd.

Front Cover: Mt Pelion West, Cradle Mountain National Park
Back Cover: Rural Scene, Central Tasmania
Facing title page: Shot Tower, Taroona

CONTENTS

General Information

HOW TO GET THERE

By air

Four out of five visitors to Tasmania reach the Island State by air. It pays to book well in advance to secure the fare you want. There are airports at Hobart, Launceston, Devonport and Burnie. Make arrangements through your travel agent. Direct numbers for bookings are: Kendall/Ansett 13-1300 and Qantas/Southern Airlines 13-1313.

By sea

The Spirit of Tasmania can carry 290 cars and can accommodate 1,290 passengers. Accommodation is also available for persons with disabilities. The overnight trip from Melbourne to Devonport in the north of the Island takes about 14 hours. Departure from Melbourne is on Monday, Wednesday and Friday and from Devonport on Tuesday, Thursday and Saturday. There are a number of different one-way fare depending on what class you want to travel and in which season. Check with your travel agent for details or ring TT-Line reservations 13 2010.

The Devil Cat, a vehicle-carrying catamaran plies between Melbourne and George Town (to the north of Launceston) during the summer holiday season. The trip takes about six hours. Departure from Melbourne is on Tuesday, Thursday and Saturday and from George Town on Wednesday, Friday and Sunday.

TOURIST INFORMATION

Tasmanian Visitor Information Centres

The staff at these centres are friendly and helpful. Pick up a copy of their free bi-monthly publication, Tasmanian Travelways, which is available at most tourist attractions, and is essential reading for a visitor. Apart from articles about the latest festivals and seasonal attractions, it has a very complete listing of accommodation throughout the State and a list of the latest bus, sea and air fares, car hire agencies, adventure activities, etc. You can find information centres in most large towns throughout the State. On 1800-806-846 you can get information about Tasmania. Here are the four major centres:

Hobart, corner of Davey and Elizabeth Streets, (03) 6230-8233
Launceston, corner of St John & Paterson Streets, (03) 6336-3122
Devonport, 5 Best Street (03) 6424-4466
Burnie, Civic Square precinct, Little Alexander Street (03) 6434-6111

Interstate holiday planning

Ring your local travel agent or a Tasmanian Visitor Information Centre in the following capital cities: Sydney, 60 Carrington Street, (02) 9202-2022 Melbourne, 259 Collins Street,(03) 9206-7922 Brisbane, 239 George Street, (07) 3405-4122 Adelaide, 1 King William Street, (08) 8400-5522 Canberra, 165-167 City Walk, (06) 9209-2122

On the Internet

At the Department of Tourism site (www.tourism.tas.gov.au) you can get a good overview of activities, regions and how to get around the State. You can use the search button to check out accommodation according to region, standard and price. "Events" takes you to a month-by-month listing of everything that is going on in Tasmania, from the Sydney to Hobart yacht race to wood-chopping to spin-ins.

Another useful government site is Tasmania Online (www.tas.gov.au/subject/tourism.htm), which has links to national parks, entertainment, as well as everything else in Tasmania.

Tasmap

Tasmap, Tasmania's official mapmaker, produces maps for every possible use for every square inch of Tasmania. These include day walk maps, tourist maps, national park maps and notes, 1:25,000 and 1:100,000 maps for the serious bushwalker — all for a reasonable price. For the tourist with a rented car, one of the best products is Tasmanian Towns Street Atlas, which seems to show every street in the whole State in a single volume.

Hobart - Service Tasmania, 134 Macquarie Street. Launceston — Henty House, 1 Civic Square.

Parks and Wildlife Service

This Government service produces valuable brochures, maps and other information about the many parks and reserves in Tasmania. A ranger is normally available to answer phone queries and help you get the most out of the national parks. You can ring on (03) 6233-8011.

Park passes

A range of national park passes lets you choose the most economical way to visit for your needs. Probably the best pass is the Holiday pass, which costs $30 per vehicle (or $12 per person) and is valid for up to two months — more than enough for your holiday. A daily rate is available at $9 per vehicle or $3 per passenger.

Royal Automobile Club of Tasmania (RACT)

The RACT has abundant information available for its members and members of affiliated automobile clubs, apart from its breakdown service, (tel: 13-2722)

Hobart, corner of Murray and Patrick Streets Launceston, corner of York and George Streets Devonport, 5 Steele Street

Burnie, 24 North Terrace

Queenstown, 18 Orr Street

Local transport

Hobart and Launceston, which have the most extensive public transport systems, nonetheless are very extensive cities. It is not a good idea to depend upon public transport if you want to visit many outlying places. In Hobart, the Metro office opposite the GPO is a good source of information about the city.

For inquiries about day tickets, family tickets, seniors' tickets and so forth, ring the Metro Hotline on 13-2201. Buses

Buses run regularly between the major towns. For further information on the timetables, ring a Tasmanian Visitor Information Centre. Special passes are available linking all the major centres and gateways to wilderness areas.

Renting a car

A car is definitely the best way to get around. If you rent a car in Tasmania rather than on the Mainland, you will avoid paying the extra cost for the ferry. There are a large number of car rental companies in Hobart, Launceston and Devonport. Consult the Tasmanian Travelways magazine for a more or less comprehensive listing of the companies and their rates for cars, motorcycles, mini-buses, trailers, campervans and caravans.

Prices for cars begin at about $20 a day plus insurance for "pre-loved" sedans. Study the fine print closely.

Most Australia-wide companies have toll-free numbers. Some Tasmanian-based companies will arrange for a car to be delivered

to you at the airport. In every city there are companies which rent
pre-loved vehicles as well - consult the Yellow Pages or Tasmanian
Travelways. It pays to shop around.

  Avis: 1800-225-533
  Budget Rent A Car: 13-2727
  Autorent-Hertz: 13-3039
  Advance Car Rentals: 1800-030-1118
  Delta Car Rentals: 13-1390
  Australian U-Drive: 1800-646-011

Travel times

Nowhere in Tasmania is too far. The Tasmanian Visitor
Information Centres estimate the following travel times for a
sedan without stopping. Use them to help plan your trips around
the State.

From/to	Hrs.Min	Kms
Launceston to Cradle Mountain	2.00	142
Launceston to St Helens via Scottsdale	2.30	169
Launceston to St Helens via Fingal	1.50	167
Launceston to Bicheno via Scottsdale	4.15	247
Launceston to Hobart via Midlands Hwy	2.10	199
Bicheno to Hobart via Sorell	2.30	182
Hobart to Port Arthur	1.25	100
Hobart to Hastings Caves	1.50	112
Hobart to Queenstown	4.00	250
Queenstown to Burnie	3.00	196
Queenstown to Devonport via Sheffield	2.40	195
Queenstown to Cradle Mountain	1.40	123
Burnie to Smithton	1.10	89
Burnie to Devonport	0.45	54
Devonport to Launceston	1.00	98
Devonport to Hobart via Midlands Hwy	3.00	278
Devonport to Cradle Mountain	1.10	81

Bed and Breakfast

Throughout Tasmania there is abundant Bed and Breakfast accommodation in refurbished colonial cottages or buildings with lots of period charm, homey decoration and warm hospitality, but without the mod cons of big new hotels. These are extremely popular. Many of them are associated with B&Bs in other cities so that you can book into a number of them around the State with a minimum of fuss. Ask your travel agent. Here are the names of some of the associations: Tasmanian Colonial Accommodation 1800-815-610 Cottages of the Colony 1800-814-603

Historic Houses of Tasmania: 1800-625-745 Tasmania's Holiday Retreats: 1800-620-487 Heritage Tasmania (in the northeast): 1800-450-030

Sport

As one of the last great wilderness areas on earth, Tasmania draws tourists from around the world eager for adventure in the rugged mountains, fast-flowing rivers and superb scenery. Many of these sports require equipment and guides. These are all available. The magazine Tasmanian Travelways has a listing of guides and tours.

White water rafting: the fiercest of Tasmania's wild rivers is the Franklin on the West Coast. In flood, adventurers from around the world test its raging waters. There is also organised rafting on the Huon and Picton Rivers, south of Hobart.

Bushwalking: there's no place on earth like Tasmania for hiking. Everywhere there are walks ranging from short strolls to lookouts, to treks lasting many days. Two of the major walking areas are the Cradle Mountain-Lake St Clair National Park and the South-West Heritage area. But even within a half-hour drive from the centre of Hobart or Launceston there are magnificent walks.

Diving: the State is establishing a system of marine reserves and there are many wrecks along the coast line for knowledgeable divers.

Skiing: Tasmania does not have world-class ski fields, but Ben Lomond, 50 km from Launceston, and Mount Field, 70 km west of Hobart, have ski tows, ski hire and other facilities. They are quite popular in a good snow season.

Fishing

Inland fishing: Tasmania is internationally renowned as one of the best trout fishing venues in the world. The clear and unpolluted waters of its streams and lakes are a delight for all anglers. Brown trout are the most common and are to be found almost everywhere, while rainbow inhabit most waters. Fine fishing is to be found less than two hours' drive from any of the major centres.

Season: Most inland waters open for trout fishing around August 1 and close around April 30. Make sure that you check the exact dates. The bag limit is 12 for most inland waters. Licences: full season: adults $45; under 14 years - no licence needed; 14-17 years $15; pensioners $25. Fourteen-day: $35. Three-day: $20. One-day: $12.

Licences are available from most sporting stores throughout Tasmania, local post offices, Tasmanian Visitors Information Centres, offices of the Inland Fisheries Commission (03) 6223-6622, and some shops and accommodation houses in the high country.

Local knowledge is obviously very important in hooking trout. With limited time, you might like to seek the services of a professional guide. Consult the Tasmanian Travelways magazine or contact the Tasmanian Professional Trout Fishing Guides Association, (03) 6289-1137. Their web site is www.fishnet.com.au/TPTGA.html.

The best locations are said to be Arthurs Lake, Great Lake and Lake Sorell, in the Midlands, north of Bothwell; Lake Pedder; Brumbys Creek, near Longford; and the Macquarie River, which flows through the Midlands. But of course, there is excellent fishing throughout the State.

Saltwater fishing: mature fin fish of all species may be caught legally throughout the year without any catch limitations, although there are some restrictions. For your copy of the code and other information, contact Service Tasmania.

The north and east coasts are favoured for saltwater fishing as the weather is milder. Tasmania's waters hold an incredible variety ranging from huge hard-fighting game fish to tasty garfish, flounder and flathead. The warm eastern Australian current draws many species which are also found much further north. Charter boats are available for hire in most parts of the state. Their operators provide the specialised knowledge and fishing skills which virtually guarantee success for the visitor.

Shopping

Opportunities to shop in Tasmania abound, but you should be prepared to search for the best bargains. Salamanca Place on a Saturday morning is a good place to start. Some of the craft shops in country areas can have a disappointingly small or idiosyncratic range of goods. The typical products to take back home are gourmet foodstuffs, wines, wood-turning with native timbers, and arts and crafts of every description. Crafts. Tasmania timber craft articles are amongst the world's best. Many are produced from the State's unique timber species, like Huon pine, blackwood, sassafras and even horizontal scrub from the wilderness rainforests. Taswegian designers and artists are leading the world with products that have won kudos in Europe and the United States.

Wines. Tasmania has emerged as one of the world's better wine regions, with its cool, temperate climate and long hours of sunshine. The number of vineyards and wineries has grown rapidly. There are now six distinct districts, each with its own soil and climate characteristics, from the Tamar Valley region near Launceston, down the East Coast to the Huon and Channel regions near Hobart. More than 25 labels are available.

Cheeses. Tasmania's long growing season and good rains have helped to create an excellent dairy industry. An amazing variety of native cheeses is available. The King Island cheeses have launched Tasmania's reputation as a gourmet's larder. Many regard them as some of the most distinctive and smooth-tasting now on the market. Soft cheese such as King Island Brie and Double Brie and Phoques Cove camembert are welcome addition to cheese platters. Lactos makes an excellent blue vein. For a real touch of luxury, try King Island's Seal Bay Creme de la Creme, cow and goat milk fetta cheese from Epicure Cheeses in Latrobe or Tasmania Gourmet Cheese's mascapone or ricotta.

FOR OVERSEAS TRAVELLERS

Entry regulations

Since Tasmania is an Australian State, all travellers there naturally need a valid passport and visa. No vaccinations are required, except for visitors from Yellow Fever endemic areas. Most travellers from overseas stop first in Melbourne or Sydney before landing in Tasmania. Before you disembark you will be given immigration forms as well as customs and agriculture declarations. As a general rule you must declare all goods of plant or animal origin. Quarantine officers will inspect these items and return them to you if no disease or pest risk is involved, although some may need to be treated first.

Consulates

Although Tasmania is Australia's smallest State, several nations have consulates or honorary consulates in Hobart. If you are not an Australian and you require diplomatic services, however, you may need to ring consulates in Melbourne or embassies or high commissions in Canberra. A few consulates are listed below:

France: 63 Salamanca Place, Hobart (03) 6231-1246
Germany: 348 Sandy Bay Road, Sandy Bay (03) 6223-1814
Italy: 151 Liverpool Street, Hobart (03) 6234-5858

Japan: 20 Utiekah Drive, Taroona (03) 6238-0200
Sweden: 164 Campbell Street, Hobart, (03) 6234-2477
Switzerland: 1 Cedar Circuit, Sandy Bay, (03) 6225-2657
United Kingdom: British Consulate-General, 90 Collins Street, Melbourne, (03) 9650-4155
United States: St Kilda Road, Melbourne, (03) 9526-5900.

Interpreters

For interpreters for all languages, there is a national 24-hour service 13-1450.

Emergencies

For fire, police and ambulance emergencies, ring 000. Medical facilities
  Hospitals, private doctors, dentists and other specialists are readily available, at least in the major centres. We recommend that overseas visitors take out accident and illness insurance cover for their visit to Tasmania.

Hospitals

Hobart. Royal Hobart Hospital, Liverpool Street, (03) 6238-8308
Launceston. Launceston General Hospital, Charles Street, (03) 6332-7111
Devonport. Mersey General Hospital, Latrobe via Devonport, (03) 6426-5111
Burnie. North-west Regional Hospital, Edward Street, Burnie, (03) 6430-6666

Driving

A current driver's licence issued in Australian States or Territories is applicable in Tasmania for 12 months. A current international driver's licence can be used in Tasmania, but it is valid only for three months.
  The speed limit in Tasmania is 60/kph in built-up areas and between "school" signs is 40/kph. Unless otherwise indicated, the

Opposite: Cascade Brewery, Hobart

maximum is 100/kph outside cities and towns with some 110/kph areas on open roads and a buffer zone of 80/kph outside of major centres. There may be no signs to remind you of the 100/kph limit, so take care! The State speed limit for "P" drivers is 80/kph. Radar speed cameras do a great job making money for the government.

In general, in a situation in which there are no signs or lights, drivers must yield to the right, except at a "T" junction, when the traffic from either direction on the through road has priority. Drivers making a right-hand turn must yield right of way to traffic approaching from the opposite direction, either proceeding straight ahead or making a left-hand turn. It is compulsory for seat belts to be worn if they are fitted to the vehicle.

If you are driving in country areas, be sure that you have enough petrol, especially at night. Stations offering 24-hour service are rare outside the major centres. And beware of wildlife crossing the road. Apart from the risk of killing native animals, you can also do your car a lot of damage.

Reading road signs

The road system in Tasmania is quite good. Many of the roads are coded with a number and the letters A, B or C. It is not a classification of road quality, but of the best way to drive from one place to another.

"A" roads, numbered from 2 to 10 are major highways. "B" roads, numbered from 11 to 99, are other important main roads. "C" roads, numbered from 100 to 999, are minor routes to features and services of interest to motorists. Some signs at intersections show a destination and a route code in brackets. This means that the destination and route do not begin at that point, but branch off further down that road.

Opposite: Tasmanian Devil

The only exception to this coding system is the National Highway from Hobart via Launceston to Burnie, which is identified by a gold number 1 on a green shield.

COMMUNICATIONS

Telephones

Public telephones are easy to find in the cities and suburbs, on street corners and in hotels, shops, cafes, etc. A local call costs 40 cents regardless of the time. If you plan to make many calls, buy a Phonecard at a newsagent or any other outlet displaying a Phonecard sign. This can be used in most Telstra phone boxes. Emergency calls are free. The area codes for each city and town have been included in this guide. The cheapest time to ring is on weekends or every day from 7pm to 7am when rates are half the day-time rate.

For international calls, you can dial direct to most countries from most phones in hotels, homes, offices or from the public phones. Simply dial 0011 + country code + area code + local number. You can find country codes in the back of the White Pages of all telephone directories. The country code for Australia is 61.

Telstra Country Direct is the easiest way of making international telephone card and reverse charge (collect) calls. When you dial your Country Direct access number, you are immediately put in touch with your own country's operator who will then connect the call. For more information, ring 1800-801-800.

Newspapers

Tasmania has three daily newspapers: the Mercury in Hobart, the Examiner in Launceston and the Advocate in Burnie. The Age, from Melbourne, and The Australian are also widely available. In Hobart, a number of foreign language publications are available at Ellison Hawker newsagents at 88-96 Liverpool Street.

Time zones

Australia is divided into three time zones: Australian Eastern Standard Time (EST), which covers the east coast of Australia - Tasmania, Queensland, NSW and Victoria - is GMT plus 10 hours.

During summer, from October to March, daylight saving is observed. However, Tasmania squeezes every day for more light and returns to EST later than the other states on the east coast. Make sure to check your time so that you do not miss your flight!

Shopping hours

Most large shops are now open all day from Monday to Saturday, 9am to 5.30pm. Corner stores open early and close late in the major centres. There are a few all-night petrol stations where you can buy some foodstuffs very late at night in Hobart. In country areas, do your shopping during the day.

Money

The Australian currency is decimal, with the Dollar as the unit of exchange. Notes come in different colours and sizes in denominations of $100, $50, $20, $10 and $5. There are $2, $1, 50-cent, 20-cent, 10-cent, and 5-cent coins. Currency exchange facilities are available at Hobart International Airport and most banks in Hobart and Launceston. You may find it difficult to change currency in country areas. Banks are normally open from Monday to Friday, 9.30am to 4.30pm. Some banks open or close a bit earlier. All banks are closed on Saturday and Sunday. Automatic Teller Machines are widely available 24 hours a day, both in cities and country towns. Banks operating both in Tasmania and on the Mainland include Westpac, ANZ, Commonwealth Bank and National Australia Bank.

Bankcard, American Express, Diners Club, Visa and Mastercard and their affiliates are widely accepted. EFTPOS is available at most supermarkets and petrol stations and a number of other outlets.

MORE GREAT THINGS TO KNOW

Electricity. Domestic electricity throughout Australia is 240 volts, AC 50 cycles. Standard three pin plugs are fitted to domestic appliances. Appliances manufactured for 110 volts, such as hair-dryers and contact lens sterilisers, cannot be used without a transformer.

Videos. VCRs operate on the PAL system.

Tipping. Tipping is not a way of life in Tasmania - or anywhere else in Australia. Of course, if you are particularly impressed by the service you have been given, you are hardly forbidden to tip. If you decide not to, however, you will not be harassed as you would be in some other countries. It is entirely up to you.

Alcohol. The legal age for purchasing alcohol is 18 years. Children are permitted into lounge bars where food is served as long as they are accompanied by an adult. Tasmanian hotels trade from 10am to 10pm from Monday to Thursday and from 10am to midnight on Friday and Saturday. These hours may differ in country areas.

The police are tough on drink drivers and one of the treats of local newspapers is reading the list of locals who have been convicted of driving under the influence. A limit of .05 is strictly adhered to. Motorists are subject to random breath testing. "P" and "L" plate drivers are not permitted to drive with any alcohol in their system. Enjoy! — but not too much.

Hobart

Hobart is the capital of Tasmania and Australia's second oldest city. It now has a population of about 190,000. It has a mild maritime climate without great extremes of temperature. In January, the hottest month, the maximum temperature is 22C and minimum is 12C. In July, the coldest month, the maximum is 11C and the minimum is 4C. There are many clear, cloudless days, but the weather can change in a matter of minutes. The suburbs of Hobart are draped over the folds and clefts of the base of the Mountain and on some days each suburb seems to have its own weather. It's not unusual for a shower or cloud of mist to dampen the footpaths and create an immense rainbow for a few minutes before the sun breaks through for the rest

of the day. In fact, since the average rainfall in Hobart is only 635 mm (25 inches), it ranks as the driest capital city in Australia, apart from Adelaide. The driest months are January, February and March, during the summer.

Seasonal changes set Hobart apart from other Australian cities. The summer is long and warm, with few really hot days. With autumn comes a burst of colour as the European trees in the gardens and parks change colour and shed their leaves. Winter is crisp and cool and the smoke from burning logs rises from chimneys throughout the city. Spring brings a burst of colour to Hobart's magnificent gardens.

INTRODUCTION

Set between the broad Derwent River and the dolomite cliffs of Mount Wellington, Hobart has one of the most spectacular settings of any capital city in Australia. The Derwent flows out to the Pacific and its deep water port has made Hobart a maritime city. In Sullivans Cove, only a few hundred metres from the heart of the city, are anchored fishing boats and the occasional cruise ship and the odd ice-breaker. Down the river, in the shadow of the spectacular Wrest Point casino, is the King of the Derwent Squadron, with hundreds of yachts. Above towers the Mountain, often swathed in cloud, and in winter capped with snow. Its dark, craggy heights with their dolomite corrugations are universally accepted as the symbol of Hobart. As you drive from the airport, its towering silhouette will be the first thing you see of the city. More than other capital cities in Australia, Hobart has preserved its colonial heritage. The place names evoke the heroes and victories of the Napoleonic wars: the battles of Salamanca and Albuera, Lord Nelson, the Duke of Wellington... The majestic public buildings of the Victorian era and the Georgian warehouses of Salamanca Place, all built in solid sandstone, stamp Hobart with its past. Like many European cities, fragments of old walls and foundations are strewn throughout the city, incorporated into modern buildings or awaiting restoration. It's not hard to imagine docks as they must have been in the days of the whalers in the 1830s and 1840s or the mining booms of the 1870s and 1880s.

The scale of Hobart is small enough to make it a dignified, personable place to live, yet large enough to have all the amenities of a thriving capital. Hobart is a provincial city, but a provincial capital city. It is relaxed, quiet, unhurried, serene and tranquil — all the adjectives for which the writers of tourist brochures have scoured their thesauruses — but not backward. On the footpaths public servants and solicitors in pin-striped suits jostle graziers and vegans with beanies and hand-knitted jumpers. It has a distinguished university and one of the world's finest small orchestras.

Hobart is the gateway to the South of Tasmania. Within an hour's drive are isolated bushland, pockets of rainforest, paddocks full of grazing sheep and cattle, sandy beaches with good surf, and historic settlements where time seems to have stopped. To the tourist's amazement, trucks laden with immense logs, some three or four feet thick, often rumble down Macquarie Street, a constant reminder of the presence of untamed bush only a few miles away. Throughout the city are shops selling camping and trekking equipment for some of the world's most unspoiled wilderness areas.

HISTORY

Before the coming of the English, the Mouheneer Aboriginal people lived in the area we now know as Hobart and they were called Niberlooner. A man named Wooraddy was the first to see the white men arrive. As the new settlement grew, however, the Aborigines slipped into the hills.

The official English settlement of Van Diemens Land took place not at Hobart itself, but at Risdon Cove, a site on the eastern shore of the Derwent. A party of 49 soldiers and convicts under the

command of Lieutenant John Bowen was dispatched from Sydney and landed in September 1803 (the exact date is a matter of dispute). The settlement was named Hobart Town after Lord Hobart, Secretary of State for the Colonies at that time. Risdon has the unhappy distinction of being the site of the first clash between the British and the Aborigines. On May 3, 1804 a group of several hundred men, women and children appeared above the camp engaged on a kangaroo drive. The soldiers panicked and opened fire, killing several of them.

Risdon Cove did not prosper and when Lieutenant David Collins arrived, he moved the settlement to Sullivans Cove on 21 February 1804. He chose the site because of its sheltered anchorage, gentle slopes and good water, which ran and still runs in a rivulet behind City Hall. The first settlers had to pick their way ashore and unload cargo from a tiny rocky outcrop which Collins had named Hunter Island. In 1820 a stone causeway was built to link it to the shore. The Old Wharf, now the area called Hunter Street, was originally the focus for all port activities in Hobart Town, although these shifted to the so-called New Wharf at Salamanca Place in the 1850s. It was there that in total about 67,000 convicts stepped ashore in Hobart after a three-month voyage from Britain. Whalers and traders from around the world were drawn to one of the best deepwater ports anywhere. The warehouses and bond stores lining Salamanca Place and the whalers' and workers' cottages in Battery Point are reminders of that boisterous era.

With the ending of transportation in 1853 and the granting of self-government in 1856, Tasmanian civic pride took the form of building splendid civic buildings such as the Town Hall and Old Government House. Hobart was the port for a prosperous agrarian economy with wool, meat, crops, fruit and timber being shipped to world markets. Nineteenth Century prosperity is still the hallmark of Hobart's architecture.

With the Twentieth Century came "hydro-electrification" and a dream of using the State's abundant water resources to produce cheap and plentiful power. This attracted many major industries to Hobart and the surrounding areas in the 40s, 50s and 60s.

However, as elsewhere in Australia, industrial manufacturing began a long decline in the 70s and efficiency came at the cost of jobs for Tasmanians. There are some Tasmanian success stories - Robert Clifford and his company International Catamarans which builds for a world market; Blundstone's, a maker of haut couture industrial footwear; and Southern Aluminium at Bell Bay, a manufacturer of car wheels. But, say local futurologists, the growth of the local economy in the new millennium will be based on service industries, such as tourism, information technology and innovative primary industry. The transition from dirt-under-your-fingernail jobs to nail-buffing jobs is not happening without pain, as the State's persistently high unemployment rate attests.

In more recent years Hobart has moved with the times without losing its vitality and historic character, although two tragedies have scarred the whole city. In 1967, after a severe drought, bushfires ravaged the city, destroying 1,293 houses and killing 62 people. The whitened skeletons of the dead gum trees can still be seen on the slopes of Mount Wellington. And in 1975, a freighter ploughed into a pylon of the Tasman Bridge. In all, twelve people died. If you look closely at the bridge's pylons, you will see that they are unevenly spaced on the eastern half, a constant reminder of the repair job. The disaster had a big impact upon the life of Hobart. Reaching Hobart became a two-hour ordeal on country roads to use a second crossing upstream at Bridgewater. Real estate prices on the eastern shore collapsed, businesses went bankrupt, families suffered and the crime rate rose by 40 per cent. As an insurance policy against another accident, the Bowen Bridge was built a few kilometres upstream.

Less visible is the community trauma after a massacre at Port Arthur in 1996. A madman began shooting everyone in sight — men, women and children — and at the end of his murderous spree thirty-five were dead. (He survived and was sentenced to life imprisonment in the State's maximum security prison.) Tasmanians were shocked that the senseless violence of distant lands had invaded their peaceful island. One positive result was national legislation to tighten up Australian gun laws, but what happened on that sunny Sunday afternoon is something which most locals would rather not talk about.

HOW TO GET THERE

(See inside back cover for map).

By air

Kendall/Ansett and Qantas/Southern Airlines both connect Hobart and Launceston with Adelaide, Brisbane, Cairns, Canberra, the Gold Coast, Melbourne, Perth and Sydney, either directly or with connecting services.

Hobart Airport is 16 km from the city centre and Redline operates a regular $7 service to the city which makes stops at the major hotels. The driver can be persuaded to drop you off at other sites as well. There always seem to be long queues of taxis waiting for a fare. A trip to the City costs about $20.

By bus

There are bus services operating in Hobart to nearly every major centre and every major wilderness gateway including Cockle Creek, Cradle Mountain, Lake St Clair, Mt Field, Scott's Peak, Strahan and the Walls of Jerusalem. You can also take bus tours of Richmond, Mt Wellington and the Channel. Consult the latest Tasmanian Travelways or the Tasmanian Visitor Information Centre for details.

By road

It is possible to travel to Hobart in less than a day from anywhere in Tasmania. The distance from Hobart in the south to Smithton on the north coast is just over 400 km, which gives you some idea of the size of the island.

Tourist information

Tasmanian Travel and Information Centre, corner of Elizabeth and Davey Streets, (03) 6230-8233, is open Monday to Friday from 8.30am to 5.15pm and on Saturdays and Sundays and public holidays from 9am to 4pm. There you can pick up many travel brochures, make tour bookings, and so on. An essential first stop.

The Wilderness Society Shop, at 33 Salamanca Place, (03) 6234-9370, has information on backpacking and trekking that its more sedate counterparts might lack, together with environmentally friendly souvenirs.

Service Tasmania, 134 Macquarie Street, (03) 6233-8011, has maps of all descriptions, as well as specialist books.

Driving in Hobart

In the central business district Hobart has an extensive system of one-way streets, arranged in a grid pattern. This is well thought out and efficient, but it can be very frustrating for a newcomer. Study your map carefully when navigating. Parking

Metered kerb-side parking is available for short-term parking. The parking officials are very observant and diligent — beware of overstaying your time.

There are a few council car parks and public car parks: North Central Car Park— entrance off Melville Street Argyle Street Car Park - between Collins and Liverpool Streets Westend Car Park — entrance off Victoria Street Wesley Car Park — 58 Melville Street

Wellington Valet Car Parking — Argyle Street Wilson Parking — Trafalgar Place, off Macquarie Street

ACCOMMODATION

The prices for accommodation vary considerably depending on the standard offered and the season. Here we provide a selection with prices for a double room per night, which should be used as a guide only. The venues are organised in rough order of price.

Wrest Point Hotel Casino, 410 Sandy Bay Road, Sandy Bay, **6225-0112.**

One of Hobart's premier venues, with views up and down the Derwent; 197 ensuites in tower, 81 ensuites in motor inn; licensed restaurants, heated indoor pool, sauna, tennis courts, mini golf. Double $200-340.

Wrest Point Casino, Sandy Bay.

Salamanca Inn, 10 Gladstone Street, Battery Point, **6223-3300.**
Within walking distance of all the sights; about 60 apartments,
licensed restaurant, heated pool, spa. Double $175-220.

Hotel Grand Chancellor, 1 Davey Street, **6235-4535.**
One of the best positions in Hobart, with views over Constitution
Dock and Derwent; 234 ensuites, licensed restaurant, bistro,
heated indoor pool, sauna, gym. Double $155-360.

Colonial Battery Point Manor, 13 Cromwell Street, Battery Point,
6224-0888.
Elegant hospitality in the heart of Hobart's historic district;
8 ensuites. Double B&B $145. Lenna of Hobart, 20 Runnymede
Street, Battery Point, 6232-3900. Close to Salamanca Place in a
distinguished colonial mansion; 50 ensuites, licensed restaurant.
Double $140-200.

Old Woolstore, 1 Macquarie Street, Hobart, **6235-5355.**
Elegantly converted buildings at the gateway to Hobart; 59
ensuites. Double $135-185.

Hobart Vista Hotel, 156 Bathurst Street, **6234-6255.**
Close to the City, with easy access to the airport; 139 units,
licensed restaurant. Double $125.

Hadley's Hotel, 34 Murray Street, Hobart, **6223-4355.**
Conveniently located right in the middle of the City with old world
charm; 63 units, restaurant. Double $110. Cromwell Cottage, 6
Cromwell Street, Battery Point. Homey charm in the historic area
of Hobart; 5 units. Double B&B $110-115.

Hobart Mid City Motor Inn, 96 Bathurst Street, Hobart,
6234-6333. In the heart of the city; 106 ensuites, licensed
restaurant. Double $98-135.

Hobart Macquarie Motor Inn, 167 Macquarie Street, Hobart, **6234-4442.**
Close to Salamanca Place and the City; 104 ensuites, licensed restaurant, pool, spa, sauna. Double $95-105.

Woolmers Inn, 123-127 Sandy Bay Road, Sandy Bay, **6223-7355.**
Easy access to the City and Battery Point; 31 apartments. Double $85-99.

Grosvenor Court Holiday Apartments, 42 Grosvenor St, Sandy Bay.
Easy access to the City and Battery Point and shops; 17 ensuites. Double $79-99.

Argyle Motor Lodge, 2 Lewis Street, North Hobart, **6234-2488.**
A bit distant from the City but easy access by car; 36 units. Room only $90-120.

Waratah Hotel Motel, 272 Murray Street, **6234-3685.**
Easy access to the City with a car; 18 ensuites, licensed restaurant. Double B&B $65.

Jane Franklin Hall, 6 Elboden Street, South Hobart, **6223-2000.**
University college near historic South Hobart with accommodation in uni holidays. Single B&B $25. Sandy Bay Caravan Park, 1 Peel Street, Sandy Bay, 6225-1264. Near the Casino and a short bus trip to the City. Double, on-site vans $35.

Treasure Island Caravan Park, Main Road, Berriedale, **6249-2379.**
About 14 km from the City, but easy car access down the Brooker Highway. Double, on-site vans $32. Adelphi Court, 17 Stokes Street, New Town, 6228-4829. A popular hostel for backpackers; room for 88. Single $14-19. Central City Backpackers, 138 Collins Street, Hobart, 6224-2404. Basic backpacker accommodation in the heart of Hobart. Single $14-30.

EATING OUT

Hobart caters for all tastes, and like any major population centre, its food outlets vary from quick takeaway to sophisticated gourmet fare. Generally speaking, the seafood dishes in the Hobart restaurants are something about which the city can boast. Check out the restaurant strip along Elizabeth Street in North Hobart for a variety of cheaper BYO international cuisine.

Lebrina, 155 New Town Road, New Town, **(03) 6228-7775.**
One of Hobart's best: lovely modern French fare in a cosy colonial setting.

The Point Revolving Restaurant, Wrest Point Casino, 410 Sandy Bay Road, Sandy Bay,
(03) 6225-0112.
Panoramic views of Hobart and the Derwent at the top of the Casino tower. Licensed. Mure's Upper Deck, Victoria Dock, 6231-1999. Great seafood and elegant dining at Victoria Wharf overlooking the boats and the Derwent River. Licensed.

Prossers on the Beach, Beach Road, Long Point, Sandy Bay, **6225-2276.**
Terrific seafood right on the Derwent. Da Angelo Ristorante, 47 Hampden Road, Battery Point, 6223-7011. Excellent Italian cuisine in a family setting.

Kelleys, Sailmakers Cottage, 5 Knopwood Street, Battery Point, **(03) 6224-7225.**
One of Hobart's premier restaurants for seafood. Warm colonial surrounds.

Seasons, 38 Cambridge Road, Bellerive, **(03) 6244-6700.**
Distinctive dining on the Eastern Shore. A perfect site, with views of yachts and the Derwent.

Blue Skies, Murray Street Pier, Hobart, **6224-3747.**
Lovely river views with your meal.

Mount Nelson Signal Station, 700 Nelson Road, Mt Nelson,
(03) 6223-3407.
A hard-to-beat spot for lunch with magnificent views over the
Derwent. Well worth the trek to the top of Mount Nelson.

The Boardwalk, Wrest Point Casino, 410 Sandy Bay Road, Sandy Bay,
(03) 6225-0112.
Good value meals overlooking the Derwent.

Mure's Lower Deck, Victoria Dock, **6231-2121.**
A terrific place for good value fish and chips and great ice creams.
Licensed.

Concetta's Pizza & Restaurant, 340 Elizabeth St, North Hobart,
6234-4624.
Homey atmosphere with good Italian cooking. BYO.

Black Buffalo Hotel, corner of Federal and Letitia Sts, North Hobart,
6234-7711.
Excellent family-style hotel with good tucker and reasonable
prices.

Chinese Palace Restaurant, 373 Main Road, Glenorchy, **6272-9911.**
A bit off the beaten track, but only a few minutes from the city.
Excellent value Chinese meals.

Tandoor & Curry House, 101 Harrington Street, Hobart,
6234-6905.
Close to the heart of the City; probably Hobart's best Indian
restaurant.

PUBS AND BARS

The social life in Hobart tends to be a pub scene with the occasional night club visit. All these places can change in tone and style so it is best to seek advice at your accommodation before venturing out. If they are not to your taste, go to the next one on the list. Here are a few suggestions:

St Ives Hotel, Sandy Bay Road, Battery Point. The most happening place in Hobart. Very popular with the younger set.

Cafe Who Bar & Bistro, 251 Liverpool Street. A very open setting with one main bar. The wooden floor and post-modern design give it character.

Nickelbys, Sandy Bay Road, Sandy Bay. An open fire with a long bar gives you the idea. A very enjoyable place for a drink with friends.

Regines Nightclub, Wrest Point Casino, 410 Sandy Bay Road, Sandy Bay. Dance floor with cover charge. Excellent variety of music.

LOCAL TRANSPORT

Bus

Metro buses depart from the central business district for the outer suburbs. Off-peak Day Rover tickets are available for about $3 and may be used between 9am-4.30pm and after 6pm on weekdays, and all day on weekends. Timetables and tickets are available at the Metro Shop in the ground floor of the GPO, 13-2201.

Bicycle Hire

Derwent Bike Hire, near the Cenotaph on weekends from 9am - from about $7 per hour, including helmet. Special concessions for families, **(03) 6268-6392** in the evening. Harley Tours of Hobart, *"The Gatehouse",* Princess Wharf No. 1, Hobart, **(03) 6224-1565.** Not quite bicycle hire, but still fun. Try a sidecar tour of the City or a trip to the top of Mount Wellington.

Car hire

Consult the Tasmanian Travelways magazine for a comprehensive list of the car hire companies and their rates for cars, motorcycles, mini-buses, trailers, campervans and caravans. Prices for cars begin at about $30 a day plus insurance for "pre-loved" sedans. If you plan to travel on unsealed roads with risk of broken windscreens or damaged duco, study the fine print closely.

SIGHTSEEING

Hobart has more than 90 buildings that have been classified by the National Trust and 63 of them are in Macquarie and Davey Streets, which run parallel to each other. Apart from those there are many other well maintained buildings still in use today. They are some of the city's most attractive features. Hobart's city centre is very close to the wharves on the Derwent and from certain vantage points, it can appear that boats are moored in the streets. The waterfront from Hunter Street, near the Grand Chancellor Hotel to Battery Point is frequented by tourists and locals alike as a picturesque place to have a stroll or a relaxing meal. The annual blue water classic, the Sydney to Hobart Yacht Race begins on Boxing Day and finishes at Constitution Dock right in the heart of the city.

The National Trust of Australia organises 2.5 hour walking tours of Battery Point on Saturdays with a morning tea included. For bookings, ring (03) 6223-7570. Adults $10, children $2.50, family $20. The tour begins at the wishing well in Franklin Square.

Another two-hour walking tour of historical Hobart starts at the Tasmanian Travel and Information Centre, 10 Davey Street. Tours in German, Dutch, French and Italian are available. For bookings, ring (03) 6230-8233. Adults $15, family $35.

Around Salamanca Place

A Saturday morning visit to Salamanca Market is a must for every visitor to Hobart. Stretching along the avenue from Davey Street to the end of Salamanca Place are scores of craftsmen, dealers in

second-hand goods, vendors of clothing, bric-a-brac, paintings, pottery, wood turning, books — just about everything! Musicians strum their guitars or hum their didgeridoos. Families with market-garden vegetables rub shoulders with hawkers of New Age crystals. It's a charming place to visit every Saturday morning until mid-afternoon, rain or shine. A great place to scoop up souvenirs for good prices or take photos of the brightly coloured umbrellas shielding the 300 stalls.

The backdrop to the markets in Salamanca Place is a picturesque row of Georgian sandstone warehouses that were built between 1835 and 1860. The so-called New Wharf which used to lie in front of the warehouses, was built of stone taken from a large quarry which can still be seen, unused. The warehouses themselves were built on the levelled land. They now house restaurants, art galleries and some offices. A terrific place for browsing or a cappuccino. One new service, Antarctic Adventure, gives you a sense of what it must be like to live in the coldest and loneliest place on the planet.

On the other side of Murray Street is the Tasmanian Parliament House opposite the wharves and is fronted by spacious lawns and gardens. The famous government architect John Lee Archer originally designed it as the local customs house. The stone for the building came from what is now a lake in the grounds of Government House. The cellars, once the bonded store, still display broad arrows on the brickwork and much of the work was done by convicts. The customs staff opened for business in 1840. The Legislative Council began meeting in the building in 1841 and it was not until 1904 that the customs officers moved to new offices in Davey Street.

Alterations allowed the House of Assembly to conduct its business there from 1856 with the advent of self-government. Visitors are encouraged to visit Parliament House whenever the House or the Council is sitting. There are guided tours on non-sitting days at 10am and 2pm. About 25,000 people visit the building each year.

Near Salamanca Place is St David's Park, the original burial ground of Hobart Town, and now a charming piece of urban greenery. The cemetery was closed in 1872 and when the area was turned into a park in 1926, many of its headstones were incorporated into the walls, gateways and the rotunda. The first to be buried there appears to have been a child who died in 1804. There are many important Tasmanian memorials here. John Lee Archer designed the monument to the first Lieutenant-Governor of Van Diemens Land, David Collins. Nearby stood the first church in Hobart Town, a wooden building which was toppled by the first winter gale. The last tribal aboriginal man, William Lanny, was buried here after he died of cholera in 1869. He had been a popular man with his whaler shipmates and his funeral was well-attended. But his grave was robbed that very night by two prominent local surgeons.

Opposite St David's Park, on Davey Street is the stone-walled Hobart Tennis Club, one of the few places in the world where you can play the ancient game of Royal Tennis. This is the only original court left in Australia.

If you walk as far as Hunter Street, near the Grand Chancellor, you can view the launching place for a financial empire that endures to this day. The fading letters "IXL" recall the years when the main industry on the Old Wharf was jam making and fruit processing. Sir Henry Jones, "Knight of the Jam Tin", created a very successful business which lasted into the 60s, when Britain's entry into the Common Market killed Tasmania's fruit trade with Europe. "I excel" became an Australian byword.

Battery Point

A stroll around Battery Point is one of the most pleasant excursions in Hobart. The suburb is named after a battery of guns established in 1818 on the promontory of land lying between Sullivan Cover in the east and Sandy Bay Creek in the west. The area has changed very little in the last 150 years—apart from the new hotels. Houses and cottages are packed into a jumble of narrow streets and lanes which gives the area a charming maritime atmosphere. The residents are very wary of any modern development.

The oldest building in Battery Point is the 1818 Signal Station which was used to relay messages from another station on Mount Nelson. News of a convict escape could be relayed from Port Arthur within a few minutes.

Near the Signal Station, at the foot of the former harbourmaster's garden is a tiny octagonal building. It was from here that the tides were measured and that all distances in Tasmania were calculated. Amongst other things, the harbourmaster was responsible for controlling smuggling and to prevent convicts from escaping.

St George's Anglican Church, on Mona Street, was also designed by John Lee Archer and built between 1836 and 1847. It has Australia's oldest classical revival spire; at night, illuminated by spotlights, it is one of the city's most prominent landmarks. The Tasmanian poet James McAuley wrote a well-known poem about the romance of an escaped convict and the church organist.

Arthur Circus is actually a quaint circular street and from around a small commons the plots of charming cottages built between 1847 and 1852 radiate out.

Narryna, on St George's Terrace, near Sandy Bay Road, is a prominent brick house with a stone facade. The simplicity of the architecture and the fountain, and the handsome ironwork of the front fence are a reminder of the elegance of the life in Hobart Town for the gentry. Narryna now houses the Van Diemen Folk Museum, which has a fascinating collection of colonial costumes, toys, paintings, china, kitchen utensils, scrimshaw, medical supplies and daguerrotypes of colonial Tasmanians. An admission fee is charged. The museum is open Tuesday to Friday 10.30 am-5 pm, and weekends and public holidays 2pm-5pm. It is closed on Christmas Day, Good Friday and Anzac Day. Admission: adults $5; concession $3.5; children $2.

Walking in the City

Franklin Square is the heart of the city, the meeting place for countless appointments and a bus depot. Throughout the day there are people playing chess at an immense board or lounging around the park. The park is dedicated to Sir John Franklin, who was Governor of Tasmania from 1837 to 1843, and afterwards died on an expedition exploring the Arctic.

Hobart's main shopping area centres on Elizabeth Mall, which stretches between the stately GPO and Liverpool Street. There are a number of specialty shops as well as large department stores where you can buy basic necessities. Only a few steps away, on the corner of Davey Street and Elizabeth Street is the main office of the Tasmanian Visitor Information Centre.

The Tasmanian Museum and Art Gallery is housed at 40 Macquarie Street and has an emphasis on Tasmanian Aborigines and early colonial activities, including the penal system. If you don't have time to visit Port Arthur or Richmond, have a look at the Museum's exhibit of the colonial penal system. There is also an outstanding collection of whaling implements and ship models. For the youngsters there are exhibits of the strange animals of Tasmania and Australia and a few dinosaur skeletons. The Museum is probably the best place to learn about the mysterious Thylacine.

The Art Gallery has a fine collection of colonial painting. It includes a number of intriguing paintings by John Glover and the tragic tableau by artist Benjamin Duterrau of Protector of Aborigines George Augustus Robinson surrounded by native Tasmanians in "The Reconciliation". The collection of modern art is not large but some of Australia's best-known artists are represented, including Emanuel Phillips, Russell Drysdale and Edith Holmes. Well worth a trip; admission is free.

St David's Anglican Church, on the corner of Macquarie Street and Murray Street, is one of the treasures of Australian church architecture. It was designed by George Frederick Bodley of London, a leading Nineteenth Century authority on Gothic architecture. The timber work is exquisite, with a floor made of Tasmanian blackwood and stringy bark and laid on a base of Huon Pine. The rood screen of English oak is one of Australia's most impressive pieces. The stained glass work is also very impressive. Its solid silver altar vessels were presented by King George III in 1803.

Around the corner, on Harrington and Macquarie Streets, is the oldest Catholic church in Hobart is St Joseph's Church, which was built in 1841. The paintings are unimpressive, but there is some fine woodwork. There are frequent services throughout the day. Curiously, the Catholic cathedral is on the outskirts of the central business district, down Harrington Street. It is a warmly charming Gothic building with some attractive modern stained glass windows. Outside, in a strange contrast with the simple Gothic exterior, is a very modern statue of the Blessed Virgin by the contemporary sculptor Tom Bass.

A bit further afield at 59 Argyle Street is the oldest synagogue in Australia. Founded in 1843, it is the only one in the world with seats set aside for convicts to worship. The numbered pews are still at the back. Amongst the convicts was a fascinating London crime boss named Ikey Solomon, who was the model for Fagin in Oliver Twist. The synagogue has the only neo-Egyptian design facade in Hobart.

The Allport Museum and Library of Fine Arts is in the State Library in Murray Street and features fine furniture, porcelain, glassware and silver dating from the Eighteenth Century, and rare and fine books. The Tasmanian Library in the same building has an extensive collection of printed material ranging from accounts of the early explorers to current publications. The W.C. Crowther Library includes an interesting collection of whaling artefacts and old medical instruments. It is open Mondays to Friday 9am-5pm and admission is free.

The Anglesea Barracks, a 10-minute walk up Davey Street, is the nation's oldest military establishment still occupied by the Army. Some of the buildings in the large complex date back to the early 1800s and the guns outside the gate were cast before 1774. It is open daily, and guided tours are held on Tuesday morning at 11am.

Away from the central business district but within easy walking distance is the Penitentiary Chapel and Criminal Courts, on the corner of Brisbane and Campbell Streets. This is one of the pearls of Tasmania's colonial architecture. The Chapel, which was used by prisoners from adjacent barracks, was designed by John Lee Archer and building commenced in 1831. In the 1860s two wings were later converted into court rooms. Spooky guided tours to this fascinating complex, which include subterranean passages, solitary cells, day holding cells and an execution yard, take place daily. Adults $7, family $19.

The Theatre Royal in Campbell Street is Australia's oldest performing live theatre. Built in the Regency style, it is a reminder of a more gracious era.

The Botanical Gardens

After a hectic morning or afternoon of sightseeing, relax at the Royal Botanical Gardens. The 13.5 hectare gardens feature Australia's widest collection of temperate climate plants. Established in 1818, it contains a tropical house, a fernery, a formal herb garden, a cactus house and a lily pond. There are sections dedicated to conifers (the largest public collection in the Southern Hemisphere), heath, Chinese plants, sub-Antarctic plants and Tasmanian plants. Its pride is a lovely Japanese garden. The kids will enjoy the **Botanical Discovery Centre,** with its interactive displays. With a touch screen you can access descriptions of plants, their common names and where they can be found in the State. Very useful for botanically-minded visitors.

Adjoining the Botanical Garden is **Government House,** the residence of Tasmania's Governor. Set on 37 acres, it is seldom open for public viewing but you can get a good look at it as you cross the Tasman Bridge. It has 73 rooms and 50 chimneys and took from 1840 to 1858 to complete. It is regarded as one of the finest vice-regal residences in Australia, with a splendid entrance hall, grand corridor and State rooms. If you happen to be in Hobart when the Governor has an Open Day, make it your business to attend.

Down Sandy Bay Road
Down Sandy Bay Road to the south is Wrest Point Casino. Now a Hobart landmark, it was Australia's first legal casino. The **John Elliott Classics Museum** is at the University of Tasmania at Sandy Bay. It contains representative examples of the art and artefacts of ancient Mesopotamia, Egypt, Greece, Etruria and Rome, ranging from 2000BC to the end of the Roman Empire. It is open from February to the end of November on Mondays, Tuesdays and Thursdays 9am-12.30pm and 1pm-5pm, and on Wednesdays 1pm-5pm.

If you'd like to have a swim in the Derwent, one of the best places is the family beach at Lower Sandy Bay. For history buffs, there is a granite monolith in the small park there which commemorates Canadians who were exiled here in 1840 after a failed rebellion.

The **Mount Nelson Signal Station** provides magnificent panoramic views of Hobart and the Derwent after a very winding trip up the flanks of Mount Nelson. It was originally established in

1811 to spot vessels entering Storm Bay and D'Entrecasteaux Channel. The signal mast, which is still standing, became a link in a chain of semaphore stations from Hobart to Port Arthur. The views are spectacular. The restaurant offers very pleasant Tasmanian fare for lunch and morning and afternoon tea.

The Tudor Court Model Village in Sandy Bay is a scale replica of a medieval English village. Created and built by John Palotta, who was crippled by polio when he was nine, it is an incredible feat of skill and loving patience. Open daily 9am-5pm. Adults $3.

The 48 metre high freestone **Shot Tower** (1870) on the Channel Highway at Taroona, is 10 km south from the centre of Hobart and is one of the principal attractions for shutter bugs. It is here that shot for rifles was made. It can be climbed via the inside steps and affords an excellent view of the Derwent Estuary. Open daily 9am-5pm. Adults $3; children $1.50.

South Hobart

Established in 1832, the **Cascade Brewery** below Mount Wellington is Australia's oldest brewery. It is open on weekdays and visitors can watch beers being produced, inspect the brewery's museum, and visit the famous Woodstock Gardens. The two-hour tours begin at 9.30am and 1pm. Bookings are essential, (03) 6224-1144. Adults $7.50, children $2.50. The sight of the brewery against the mountain is worth a snapshot as you travel up Cascade Road.

For a family picnic close to the city, the **Waterworks** is the place — a beautiful grassy park overlooking a reservoir shaded by lofty gum trees. It is a Hobart favourite. While you are there, spare a moment to investigate the **Receiving House Museum,** the ruins of a water supply station which have been transformed into a monument to late 20th Century political correctness.

Mount Wellington

No visit to Hobart would be complete without visiting Mount Wellington. The drive to the summit will take you about a half-hour. Drive up Davey Street, bear right onto the Huon Road towards Fern Tree and follow the signs. Half-way up there is a viewing station over the Huon Valley and Bruny Island which is worth a few snaps. Further on, the road winds past "the Springs", the ruins of a hotel which was burnt down by several bush fires and finally abandoned, and then below the Organ Pipes, the immense dolomite cliffs which give the mountain its rugged character. Towards the top, past the tree line, there are tall poles painted white and capped with orange to mark the road in heavy snowfalls. If you clamber to the top of the rocks surmounted by a trig station, you will be standing on 1,270 metres of rock.

At the top, and out of the wind in the viewing station, you can get a superb view of Hobart and beyond for up to 100 km away, if the weather is on your side. Always take a jumper with you for it can get quite cool even in summer when it is buffeted by wind and a chilly mist. In winter the mountain is often dusted with snow and sometimes the road is closed off. After a weekend snowfall, you will see car after car descending the mountain with a snowmen mounted on their bonnets. Sometimes enthusiastic children (and adults) pelt passing cars on the way up with snowballs. There are many tracks up Mount Wellington. If you are interested in doing a walk, pick up the Tasmap publication, "Mt Wellington Walks Map and Notes".

Travelling north

The historic home Runnymede in Bay Road, New Town, to the north of Hobart, was built in 1844. It was a family home from that time until 1967. It is now managed by the National Trust and has been set up as a gentleman's residence of the 1840-60 period. It is open for inspection daily 10am-4.30pm, except Good Friday, the month of July and Christmas Day. A $5 admission fee is charged.

Off the beaten track in Lenah Valley is the rather bizarre sight of a small Greek temple surrounded by gum trees. The Lady Franklin Museum was built early in the 19th Century and nowadays it is the headquarters of the Art Society of Tasmania. It has a display of paintings by Tasmania's leading artists and a library of art books. It is open on Saturdays and Sundays 1.30-4.30pm and admission is free.

The Tasmanian Transport Museum is in Anfield Street, Glenorchy. It features steam locomotives, rail cars, road vehicles, old trams and so on. On the first Sunday of each month there are rides on a diesel rail car and on the third Sunday on a steam train. The museum is open on Saturdays and Sundays and most public holidays, 1pm-5pm. It is closed on Christmas Day and Good Friday. An admission fee is charged on train ride days.

At Moorilla Estate at Berriedale about 15 minutes' drive north of the city, you can stop to taste the best of Tasmanian wine and food. Moorilla is Tasmania's first modern-day commercial vineyard.

The **Chocolate Factory Tours** at Cadbury Schweppes in Claremont, a few minutes' drive north along the Brooker Highway, is one of Hobart's most popular. This is Australia's largest confectionary manufacturing plant, and covers some 100 hectares. There is a lot of walking. The tours include chocolate samples and an opportunity for confectionary bargains. Chocoholics beware! Book a tour on 1800-627-367. They take place Monday-Friday at 9am, 9.30am, 10.30am, 11.15am (with a cruise) and 1pm. Adults $10; children $5; pensioner concession $7; family $25. Cadbury's is closed on public holidays and factory shutdown times.

The Alpenrail will please the most demanding train buff. It is the largest and most realistic model railway in Australia, and brings to Tasmania the scenic charms and incredible engineering feats of the Swiss Alps. Children can operate some of the smaller railway layouts. Open Wednesday to Sunday 10am-4.30pm from September to June, and daily during January and February. Adults $4.50 and children $2. If you are interested in investigating Tasmanian animal life, the **Bonorong Park wildlife centre** on Briggs Road in Brighton, about 25 minutes from Hobart, is the place to go. It features wombats, koalas, Tasmanian devils and free-ranging kangaroos in a pleasant park setting. At the Bush Tucker Shed you can buy billy tea and damper, as well as other traditional Aussie food. Adults $7.50, children $4, (03) 6268-1184.

The Eastern Shore

The Eastern Shore of Hobart is seldom frequented by tourists, but you can get stunning photographs of Mount Wellington, the CBD and the Derwent from various vantage points. Rosny Lookout is a great spot for photos. The Bellerive Battery, further south, was built in the 1880s when a Russian invasion was feared. The massive walls, the surrounding moat, underground galleries and gun emplacements complete with several original guns are in good order. It's a great place for kids to explore. From the Fort you have excellent views of the Derwent and Mount Wellington.

The Bowen pyramids in Risdon Cove Historic Site commemorate the first settlement of the British in Tasmania. If you are keen to go surfing, Hobart's best surfing beach is Clifton Beach, about 45 minutes' drive from the city. The water is normally quite warm in the summer.

Cruising on the Derwent

A ferry service, the M.V. Emmalisa, crosses the Derwent from Brooke Street Pier to Bellerive Wharf on Mondays to Fridays. The trip takes about 15 minutes and is timed for commuters from the Eastern Shore. The cost is $1.20 for adults and 60cents for children. It's a cheap way to have a good look at the city. For details (03) 6223-5893.

At Brooke Street Pier a number of two-hour cruises up and down the Derwent are available both mornings and afternoons.

RICHMOND

Richmond is as elegant today as it was in the 1820s when it was an important military post and convict station linking Hobart with Port Arthur. Situated only 27 km north of Hobart on the Coal River, its village green is shaded by leafy green trees, and its old stone buildings house galleries, tea shops, craft boutiques and museums. It is one of Tasmania's most popular tourist attractions. If you don't have time to visit the stark penal settlement of Port Arthur or the picturesque Georgian buildings of the Midlands, try Richmond — it has a bit of both. The town owes its lack of development to the fact that it declined after the Sorell Causeway was opened in 1872 and Port Arthur traffic no longer had to pass its way.

The northern section of Richmond Gaol was built in 1825 — five years before Port Arthur — to house gangs of convicts working locally and for prisoners in transit. It is probably the oldest surviving convict gaol in Australia and is much the same at it was at the height of its development in 1840. The Goal is open daily 9am-5pm except Christmas Day and Good Friday. Admission $3; children 6-16 $1.50; family $7.50.   The gaol once held the bushranger Martin Cash. Izzy Solomons, a notorious London brothel-keeper, swindler and fence, who is thought to have been the original Fagin from Oliver Twist, was also a guest there. The men's solitary cells, each about two metres by one metre, and the flogging yard, with its thick, high walls, are terrifying places for anyone with a vivid imagination. There are also interesting artefacts from colonial times on display.

The charming Richmond Bridge spanning the Coal River was built by convicts in 1823 to 1825, making it the oldest bridge still in use in Australia. The "flagellator" of the 1830s, George Glover, was murdered by convicts who threw him from the bridge when he was drunk. A local legend says that his ghost still haunts the bridge. With the possible exception of Sydney's coat hanger, it is probably the most photographed bridge in Australia. The willows and poplars, the riverbank lawns and waddling ducks make it a perfect place for a family picnic.   Framed by the arches of Richmond Bridge, on a knoll rising above the Coal River and its willows and poplars one can see the oldest Catholic Church in Australia. St John's Catholic Church was built in 1836. Some additions were made in 1859, but since that time there have been very few alterations. The blackwood altar is a fine piece of local work. The cemetery surrounding the church gives a sense of the suffering of the early colonists. One small grave beside the entrance to the church deserves some explanation. Buried there is the infant son of Thomas O'Meagher, one of the famous Irish rebels transported for their part in the 1848 insurrection. He settled in Ross, where he married an Irish lass whom he had rescued when her buggy overturned. When he managed to escape to the United States in 1852, he left behind his pregnant wife. Their child died when only a few months old. When she heard that her husband was safe in the United States, she sailed for Ireland, but died before they could be reunited. O'Meagher went on to become a Union general in the Civil War and eventually governor of the territory of Montana. St Luke's Church of England is another striking convict-built building designed by John Lee Archer. It was finished by about 1835. The fine stonework of the exterior has survived virtually unchanged to the present day and there is some lovely stained glass work. On your right as you leave the church is the old Rectory, a superb example of colonial Georgian architecture. It was built in 1830 by Captain James Gordon, who gave his name to the Gordon River on the West Coast.

Probably the best way to spend your visit to Richmond is a walk up and down the main street. Scattered along it are restored sandstone cottages, many of them now selling craft and antiques. Many of the other buildings in Richmond are of great historic interest.

The Richmond Maze and Tea Rooms, Bridge Street, are open daily 10am-5pm. The labyrinth of passageways eventually leads to two surprise centres. Great fun for the kids. Adults $3.50; children $2.50; family $11.

The award-winning *Old Hobart Town Model Village* depicts Hobart as it was in the 1820s. It is a trip into the past when Hobart Town was a bustling port of more than 3000 people. Adults $6; children $3.

Eating out

Most of the eating places in Richmond are coffee shops and tea rooms catering for people out for an afternoon stroll around the town. But there are a couple of good restaurants:

Prospect House, Richmond Road, **(03)6260-2207.**
Top-flight cuisine in a charming Georgian mansion.

Richmond Arms, Bridge Street, **(03) 6260-2109.**
Very pleasant bistro meals for the family.

Accommodation
If you wish to stay overnight there are a number of establishments in Richmond.

Prospect House, Colebrook Main Road, **(03) 6262-2207.**
Premier accommodation, 11 ensuites, licensed restaurant. Double $104-116.
Richmond Country B&B, 472 Prossers Road, **(03) 6262-4238.**
 Double B&B $75.
Emerald Cottage, 23 Torrens Street, **(03) 6262-2192.**
Double B&B $124-132.
Richmond Cabin & Tourist Park, 48 Middle Tree Road,
(03) 6262-2192.
Caravan double $32-38.

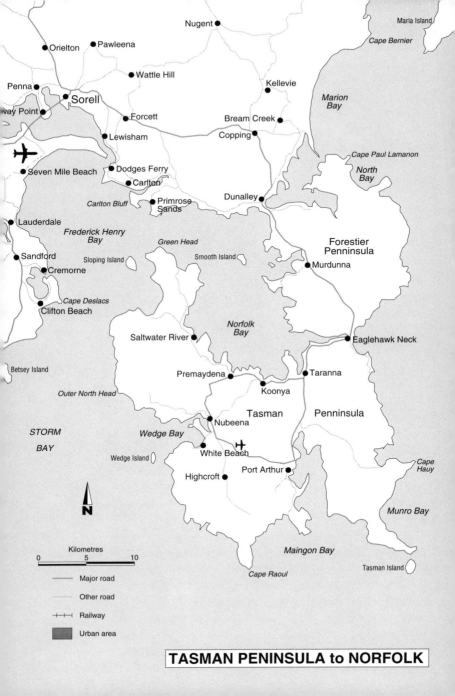

TASMAN PENINSULA to NORFOLK

Port Arthur and the Tasman Peninsula

Port Arthur, Tasmania's premier tourist attraction. It lies about 100 km south-east of Hobart on the Tasman Peninsula, a rugged, hilly chunk of land which dangles from another peninsula, the Forestier Peninsula. Although most tourists only take a day trip from Hobart to Port Arthur, you could easily spend several days in the area. Apart from the immense site of Port Arthur there are other, less well-known ruins on the Tasman Peninsula which are well worth visiting, camping sites and bushwalks with spectacular vistas of the Southern Ocean.

Today Port Arthur is a beautiful picnic spot, with vast lawns and sandstone ruins sprawling over 40 hectares, a sort of Australian Angor Wat rescued from encroaching eucalypts. But from 1830 to 1877 it was a prison for about 12,500 convicts from across the British Empire. Despite its rugged beauty with dense forests, surf beaches and precipitous sea cliffs, the Tasman Peninsula was probably a chilly, damp and forbidding place of exile for them. Escape was rare and many convicts remained to be buried in mass graves on the Isle of the Dead. After the settlement was closed as a prison, a succession of bushfires ravaged many of the buildings, but in recent years archaeologists and historians have stabilised or restored many of them so that Australians can understand their convict past.

HOW TO GET THERE

By bus

You can take an organised tour run by Experience Tasmania which departs from Brooke Street Pier on Monday, Wednesday, Friday and Sunday at 9.15 am and returns a 5 pm. Adults $45, children $30 (includes the entry to Port Arthur). Bookings on **(03) 6234-3336** or ring the Tasmanian Visitor Information Centre on **(03) 6230-8233.**

Tigerline runs daily tours to Port Arthur which depart from the Transit Centre at 199 Collins Street. Adults $45. The trip includes a look at geological features along the way. Tigerline also offers a $55 trip which includes the Bush Mill as well. Details on **(03) 6231-2200.**

By road

From Hobart, take the A9 to the Airport and Sorell and thence to Port Arthur. It takes about 11/2 hours.

Tourist information

Port Arthur Historic Site, **(03) 6250-2363** or Tourism Tasmania Offices, **(03) 6230-8233.**

ACCOMMODATION

There are quite a few motels and hotels on the road to Port Arthur, and as it can be visited in a day from Hobart there is no problem ensuring you have a bed for the night. The quality of the accommodation varies. Here we have a selection, with prices for a double room per night, which should be used as a guide only.

Port Arthur Motor Inn, Remarkable Cave Road, **(03) 6250-2101,** 35 ensuites, licensed restaurant, double $110. Fox and Hounds Motor Inn, Arthur Highway, **(03) 6250-2217,** 28 ensuites, licensed restaurant, playground, swimming pool, tennis court, games room, double $70-135. Port Arthur Caravan and Cabin Park, 1 km north of historic site, (03) 6250-2340, cabin double $50-70, hostel double $22-26.

Port Arthur Youth Hostel, Champ Street, **(03) 6250-2311,** dormitory accommodation with kitchen and shower facilities, $13-16 per person.

SIGHTSEEING

Port Arthur Historic Site. The former port and prison is open every day except Christmas, 9am-5pm. The entrance fee is: adults $16, children 4-18 $8, family $38, concession $12.80. The entrance fee includes a harbour cruise, very informative walking tours and access to all of the buildings. The tickets are valid for 24 hours, but if you intend to return at any time in the next year, convert it into a non-transferable annual pass at the museum at no extra cost (except in June, July and August). Guided tours leave all day on the half hour, or you may wish to hire a walkman and ramble around by yourself. The guides are very knowledgeable and if you have time, it is well-worth while tagging along with one of them. It is wise to take an umbrella and rain gear, as showers often sweep through the area. For information, ring **1800-659-101.** The new visitors' centre has a number of features which will help the kids enjoy their trip to Port Arthur. The nightly Ghost Tour has become one of the most popular features of Port Arthur. This 1.5 to 2 hour tour takes place at 8.30pm each evening (9.30pm in daylight saving time) except December 24 and 25. Adults $12, children 4-17 $8, family $32. It departs from the visitors centre. Very scary! Bookings required; ring **1800-659-101.**

Port Arthur is the pre-eminent symbol of Australia's convict heritage. It was established there because of the abundance of good timber with a safe port. The settlement operated from 1830 to 1877 as a timber-producing "sawing station" and also as an industrial prison. From about **1834 to 1848** it operated as a full-scale ship-building industry and more than 200 boats were built there, probably a constant temptation for convicts to escape.

Many of the convicts were multiple offenders, but some were famous political prisoners. Early conditions were harsh, although they compared favourably with other institutions in the British

Empire. In many ways Port Arthur represented a step towards the development of the modern prison system. In the 1860s, after the cessation of transportation, it became a depot for paupers and lunatics, who eventually outnumbered the healthy convicts. Administrative control passed to the colonial government. In 1877, Port Arthur was closed as a prison and became a popular tourist destination. Many of the buildings were auctioned off to private buyers and converted into guest houses or hotels. The township was renamed Carnarvon to erase the stain of the convict past. Unfortunately, bushfires virtually destroyed it in 1895 and 1897, leaving brick and stone shells of many of the magnificent buildings. Vandalism became a problem. Nowadays, only two out of perhaps 300 wooden buildings are left. Amongst the curiosities of Port Arthur is its claim to Australia's first railway — but powered by the feet of convicts, not pistons of engines. Across the seven relatively flat kilometres from Norfolk Bay and Port Arthur, split gum log sleepers were laid with timber rails. Each rough wooden wagon was propelled by four convicts and could sometimes reach 50/kph on downhill runs. The journey took between 30 and 45 minutes. The line became uneconomic with the development of steamships and was closed in 1858.

There were also several subsidiary establishments on the peninsula: the Coal Mines, the Saltwater Agricultural Station, timber mills at Premaydena and Koonya and the guard posts at Eaglehawk Neck and Dunalley.

Point Puer, the boys' prison, is across the bay. Here lads between the ages of eight and eighteen served after being convicted of crimes in Ireland or England. Still left are ruins of the bakers' ovens and the old school. Semaphore stations were located on line-of-sight around the Peninsula and up to Hobart. (It took about 15 minutes to send routine messages to Hobart.)

Port Arthur has always had a special place in the Australian psyche. Its popular image as a cesspit of cruelty and depravity fostered by the melodramatic excesses of Marcus Clarke's 1874 novel For the Term of His Natural Life was not really deserved, as brutal punishments like flogging eased in the 1840s and 1850s. (The prison on Sarah Island in Macquarie Harbour, however, was truly a hellish place.) Even in the last century, people began to recognise that Port Arthur was a national treasure, a window on Australia's grim birth as a convict outstation. In recent years, an enormous amount of effort has gone into making it a place of national pilgrimage.

Some of the more interesting buildings are described below, but all are worth investigating.

Lunatic Asylum, Museum and Gift Shop. This brick building with an impressive clock tower was once the lunatic asylum for the mentally ill, although refurbishments have altered its original design. As Port Arthur aged, so did the convicts. It was finished in about 1867 and was intended to accommodate about 100 patients. It was divided into 20 separate rooms with large amusement and recreation area. The insane or senile were not treated badly, but not with skill or great kindness either. As the Hobart Mercury noted in 1877, "if an inmate behaves himself well he is tolerated; if he is noisy he is controlled; and if he dies there is an end of him." The building now contains an audio-visual theatre, a scale model of Port Arthur up to the 1870s, and a shop with souvenirs, posters, etc. The museum displays are impressive, with real leg irons and flogging whips which gives an idea of the suffering of the prisoners — and sometimes of their guards. There are records of the transportees sent to Tasmania with their crimes and punishments. The minimum term of transportation was seven years, which was imposed for such offences as stealing a lamb, a sheep, a pig. One prisoner, Joseph Parker, was transported for life for stealing a silk handkerchief. On another list, several men and women were sentenced to transportation for life for theft of articles of little value. In one case, the sentence of death for stealing 24/- was commuted to transportation for life. Even children received long gaol sentences.

The Model Prison

In the 1840s the fashionable punishment for difficult cases was the "separate system" of prison discipline, in which prisoners ate well, received humane treatment from the wardens, lived in clean and ventilated cells and were given adequate exercise. But they were deprived, as far as possible, of all human contact. The Model Prison at Port Arthur was copied from Pentonville Prison in England, down to its imported fittings. There are 50 cells, arranged in three wings, which radiate from a central hall, and a fourth wing with the Chapel. Whenever they left their cells for exercise, they had to wear a mask to conceal their identity and they were not to communicate with other prisoners. The restored Chapel gives you some idea of this ghastly, spirit-breaking way of dealing with hardened prisoners. It must be one of the most depressing monuments to bureaucratic boobydom in all Australia, with its separate compartments designed to allow the convicts to gaze straight ahead and only at the preacher. Only during the hymn singing in Chapel services could the prisoners exercise their vocal cords. The Model Prison's dumb cells, with windowless, walls nearly a metre thick, which are entered through an outer door and three inner doors, are frightening and eerie. What they must have done to men in solitary confinement is hard to grasp, except perhaps for people who listen regularly to Parliament on radio.

The Penitentiary

This impressive building is the largest at Port Arthur, and at one stage it may have been the largest in the colony. Originally it was a flour mill and granary powered by the mill race nearby and a convict-powered treadmill. At full production the four-floor granary held about 300,000 bushels of grain and when both wheels were working, about 18 bushels could be ground in an hour. It took five years to build — and operated for about as long before it became obsolete. This may have been because there was seldom enough water to work the wheel. Even in the 19th Century they knew how to build white elephants!

By 1857 the building had been converted into a penitentiary, with scores of separate apartments, a lofty entrance-hall, a spacious dining room, a Roman Catholic chapel, and on the top floor a dormitory with 348 bunks. Contemporary records describe it as an elegant and imposing structure.

The Church

The ruin of the colonial Gothic church has become a symbol of Tasmania itself, a beautiful structure designed with simple grandeur. Although the architect of the church is unknown, convict architect Henry Laing did the drawings in 1836. During the excavations, one of the convicts was murdered by a fellow-prisoner. The foundation stone was laid in 1836 and it was completed in 1837. The plan was somewhat unorthodox with an altar in its centre. The pulpit was behind it, in front of the tower. At services, there would have been up to 1000 convicts sitting in the western wing and 200 officials and their families in cushioned,

curtained-off pews along the eastern wall on either side of the pulpit. A spire was added in about 1842, but it was blown down by a heavy wind in 1876 and never replaced. In 1884 a fire destroyed the roof, all the structural timbers and all the internal fittings. The church was always recognised as an important historical monument and as early as 1914 the Public Works Department began a long process of conservation.

Today you can walk through the sandstone ruins and climb the restored tower and imagine convicts worshipping below every Sunday under the stern scrutiny of their warders. Religion was an important element in the penal system of Port Arthur, for no prisoner was considered reformed unless he had repented of his crimes against God and man. Initially the established church, the Church of England, could find no Anglican clergy willing to serve at Port Arthur, so a Wesleyan minister was appointed in 1833. In 1842 an Irish Catholic prisoner stubbornly refused to attend Protestant Sunday services. Eventually to the consternation of the Government, all 185 Catholic prisoners refused to attend and a Catholic chaplain was appointed. In the last three decades of the prison settlement, Protestants and Catholics used the church at different times. For this reason, it was never officially consecrated.

Government Gardens
The serene walk from Government Cottage near the Church down to the parking lot takes you through an authentic 19th Century garden. Care has been taken to ensure that the plants are those which might have been tended by colonial gardeners.

The Isle of the Dead
A few hundred metres offshore is the last resting place of 180 military and civilian personnel and 1769 convicts and paupers. A boat leaves the jetty regularly for a 40-minute guided tour of the island. This is one of the highlights of a visit to Port Arthur and well worth the $6 admission. Free settlers were buried on a little knoll, their graves marked by massive headstones with

inscriptions cut by convict masons. The convicts were interred in lower ground, six or seven in an unmarked grave. The most famous person resting here is Henry Savery, notorious forger and Australia's first published novelist, the author of Quintus Servinton, an autobiographical account of his own downfall and travails, with the hero ending his days happily in Devonshire, instead of a lonely, savage prison camp. A memorial stone was erected in 1992 by the Tasmanian literary community.

O'Brien's Cottage

Not all of the prisoners at Port Arthur were criminals whose lives have been forgotten by history. William Smith O'Brien was a political prisoner so prominent that he was treated to his own cottage. O'Brien was a member of the British Parliament for 17 years and a leader of the Young Ireland Movement. In 1848 he sought to rally a rebellion against British rule. It was quickly crushed and O'Brien and three fellow conspirators received a death sentence, which was commuted to transportation for life. Unlike the others, he refused to give his word that he would not escape. At Port Arthur he was confined in his movements, but corresponded widely with people in the Colonies and Britain. He finally accepted a ticket-of-leave in 1850 and left Van Diemen's Land in 1854.

Medical Officer's House

This house and its furnishings have been restored to the way it looked in convict days and is now an award-winning museum. Built in 1847 to 1848, it served as the Medical Officer's house until the early 1870s when it became successively a private residence, a guest house and a hotel.

OTHER SITES ON THE TASMAN PENINSULA

Tasman Monument

Just before you cross to the Forestier Peninsula, is the small town of Dunalley, once named East Bay Neck. A simple monument marks the spot where Europeans first stepped on Australian soil, on December 2, 1642. Abel Tasman's ships, Heemskirk and Zeehan anchored offshore and a few of his sailors ventured ashore to look for water and food. It is a shame that such a significant site is not better marked.

Doo Town

This well-known group of holiday houses has always fascinated Australians. Most of the houses have names incorporating "Doo", such as Much-a-Doo, Didgeri-Doo, Doo Little or Doo Me.

Eaglehawk Neck

As you drive over the winding ups-and-downs of the road to Port Arthur, you come to a narrow isthmus linking the Forestier Peninsula to the Tasman Peninsula. Between 30 and 40 men and up to 18 savage dogs were stationed there to prevent convicts from escaping from the penal settlement. Lamps were hung outside the dogs' kennels and cockle shells were strewn on the ground to reflect the light. Dogs were even placed on stages out in the water to detect swimming prisoners. A small settlement grew up there (on the Hobart side of the dog-line). The Officers' Quarters is the oldest surviving timber military building in Australia.

Tessellated Pavement

At Eaglehawk Neck is a shelf of rock which looks like well-laid large pavers. Nearby are several coastal formations - the Devil's Kitchen, Tasman's Arch and Blowhole. These natural formations are well worth a visit. They are unique in Australia.

Tasmanian Devil Park

Off the main highway to Port Arthur, about 9 km from Eaglehawk Neck near the town of Taranna, is a small wildlife park which harbours injured and orphaned native animals. If you are making a quick visit to Tassie, it is an excellent place to see live Tasmanian Devils, quolls, wedge-tailed eagles, echidnas, wallabies, kangaroos and potoroos. There are plenty of photo opportunities in a paddock with grazing wallabies. The park is open daily except Christmas Day, 9am-5pm (later in summer) and admission is $8 adult, $4 child, $22 family.

Coal Mines Historic Site

Not as well developed, but just as historic as Port Arthur is Tasmania's first operational mine, past Saltwater River in the north-western part of the peninsula. It was worked by convicts from 1834 to 1848. At one stage nearly 200 men lived there as convict miners or soldier supervisors. The main shaft reached almost 100 metres, with an extensive system of subterranean tunnels and caves. Mines in the convict days served a dual purpose. They provided fuel for use in the colony, and were used as a punishment centre. In producing 80 tons daily the convicts were basically worked to death here. Cells were even built into the mine galleries. The government sold the mine to private interests in 1848 because it was uneconomic and because of the government's concerns about homosexual behaviour. Today there are a number of imposing sandstone ruins. They were abandoned in 1877 after an underground fire.

Fortescue Bay

A popular camping spot about 10 km off the main highway. Beginning at the bay is a three to four hour walk to magnificent views from Cape Hauy at the summit of towering cliffs.

The Bush Mill Steam Railway and Pioneer Settlement, one kilometre before Port Arthur, this tourist development depicts the timber industry at the turn of the century. The narrow gauge railway twists down a 35 metres hillside, taking passengers on a scenic four kilometre journey. (03) 6250-2221. Admission fee including a train ride is $12 for adults; $6 for children between 3 and 16; and $32 for families.

Remarkable Cave

Another blowhole which, unlike the Devil's Kitchen formation, is accessible at low tide. This is seven kilometres south of Port Arthur, and an after-dinner walk there reveals spectacular coastal scenery and 300 metre high sea cliffs. Large binoculars have been placed at the car turning circle. The scenery at Cape Raul is quite spectacular as years of weathering have caused the rock to split vertically, creating an organ pipe effect.

South of Hobart

In 1772 a French expedition of two ships anchored in a channel between the Tasmanian mainland and an island, in the belief that it was the mouth of the Derwent River. In command were Admiral Bruni D'Entrecasteaux and Captain Huon Kermandec. They did not stay long, but a year later they returned and explored the Huon River by whaleboat. Their names and the name of their ships, the Recherche and the Esperance, are commemorated on Tasmanian maps today. The drive along the coast makes a pleasant country outing.

Bruny Island and the D'Entrecasteaux Channel
Kingston-Blackmans Bay

The Southern Outlet (A6) from Hobart leaves you at a turn-off for Kingston and Blackmans Bay within about 20 minutes — an area which is one of Hobart's fastest growing outer suburbs. It has attractive beaches (little surf) and picnic areas. Blackmans Bay has a small blowhole, and lookouts at Doughty Point and Piersons Point offer superb views of Bruny Island and Storm Bay.

Kingston is also home to the headquarters of **Australia's National Antarctic Program.** A public display gives visitors a greater understanding of Australia's involvement in Antarctica and the Southern Ocean. You can buy a wide range of Antarctic gifts,

Bruny Island Lighthouse

posters, postcards and other souvenirs in the cafeteria. The display is open Mon-Fri 8.30am-5pm. (The only Australian owned and operated ice-breaker, the dark orange-coloured *Aurora Australis,* is often berthed in Hobart in between trips to Antarctic bases for research and resupply. It breaks ice 1.2 metres thick at a steady rate of 2.5 knots and can carry 24 crew and 109 expeditioners.)

Margate

About 20 km from Hobart, Margate has a motor museum and an unusual market, with headquarters in Tasmania's last passenger train. The converted carriages house toy-makers, glass blowers, woodworkers, artists and other craft makers. From the main street on a clear day, you can take a lovely photo of Mount Wellington from a quite unfamiliar angle.

Snug

A few kilometres further south on the Channel Highway, Snug is a small village which was terribly damaged in the 1967 bushfires. The Channel Historical and Folk Museum is worthwhile visiting. Blocks of freestone cut at Snug were used in building the Melbourne Post Office.

A walk to Snug Falls makes a good family excursion. Turn west onto Snug Tiers Road; branch off onto Snug Falls Road and drive about three kilometres up to a car park. The track slopes down for just over a kilometre. Even young children can clamber down without much trouble. At the end are 20 metre falls surrounded by tree ferns. They are especially impressive after a good rainfall.

BRUNY ISLAND

A little further down the road is the fishing town of Kettering and the terminal for the Bruny Island vehicular ferry. What Tasmania is to the Mainland, Bruny Island is to Tasmania. It is a popular holiday spot for Hobartians and once there, you are well and truly away from it all. With an area of 362 square kilometres, Bruny is Tasmania's fourth largest island. (Keep an eye out for the *forty-*

spotted pardalote, one of Australia's endangered species, which still survives in reasonable numbers in small colonies on Bruny. It is a light olive-coloured bird about 10 centimetres long with pale yellow around the eye and on the rump and distinctive white dots along its back wings.)

A narrow sand spit links North Bruny, with its open paddocks and drier climate, with South Bruny, with its steep hills and rain forest. South Bruny has more to offer for the tourist. It has a wonderful combination of spectacular cliff views, sandy beaches, rain forest bushwalks, wildlife and historical visits. Although the main roads are sealed, there are long unsealed sections. There are small shops and tea houses, however it might be an idea to pack a picnic lunch if you plan to travel throughout the island in a single day. It takes only 15 minutes from Kettering to reach North Bruny on the *Mirambeena,* a modern vehicular ferry with a carrying capacity of 70 cars. If you visit on a weekend or public holiday, bear in mind that the queues for the ferry can be very long. Arrive at the wharf with plenty of time to spare. The return fare for the ferry per car is $18 to $23.

ACCOMMODATION

There are a number of cottages and caravan parks on Bruny, but they are small. Make sure that you book ahead as they fill up quickly.

Mavista Spa Cottages, Adventure Bay, **(03) 6293-1347**
Double B&B $90-125.

Adventure Bay Caravan Park, Adventure Bay, **(03) 6293-1270**
Caravan double $30.

Bruny was the birthplace of Truganini, the last of the Aboriginal Tasmanians. She was the daughter of Mangana, chief of the Nuenonne tribe. Most of the members of her family died at the hands of white men, but she joined George Robinson in his mission as a conciliator and twice saved his life. The last of her five husbands was William Lanny, the last Tasmanian Aboriginal male.

She died in 1876 and her skeleton was displayed for many years in the Hobart Museum, but in 1975 her remains were cremated and the ashes scattered in the channel off Bruny. A memorial to her was placed on the summit of the sand dunes at Neck Beach, but it has been vandalised and only the rock base remains, a melancholy emblem of the fate of the first Australians. The Aborigines called their island Lunawannaalonna and the name lives on in the townships of Lunawanna and Alonnah.

Bruny is rich in European history as well. James Cook, Tobias Furneaux, Bruni D'Entrecasteaux, Matthew Flinders and William Bligh all made landfall at Adventure Bay, on the Pacific side of the Island. The botanist on Captain Cook's 1777 expedition took the first samples of Australia's unique flora for Europeans to examine. Timber from Bruny was renowned for its size and quality and was used to build wharves in South Africa and England. From about 1820 to 1850, Bruny was part of the thriving whaling industry and supported a permanent whaling station with 80 residents. Nowadays, it is a very quiet place, with a handful of tiny villages and some holiday settlements. (Hotel Bruny in Alonnah claims to be Australia's most southern hotel.)

Bruny can easily take up a full day's touring and you might be tempted to stay overnight. Some of the more interesting sites are:

The Neck

The 100-metre strip of towering dunes joins the two Brunys. It is also a wildlife sanctuary where you can see fairy penguins and muttonbird rookeries from the stairway or the observation deck. During the nesting seasons (September to February for fairy penguins and September to April for muttonbirds) you can watch them returning to their burrows at dusk. Neck Beach is suitable for swimming, although there is a small rip.

Mount Mangana

You can drive from Adventure Bay to Lunawanna across Mount Mangana, which has some wonderful views and thick rainforest growth. The winding road is unsealed and can be slippery in wet weather.

Cape Bruny Lightstation

Following three major shipwrecks in this area in 1835, John Lee Archer was commissioned to design the 13-metre lighthouse. It went into use in 1838 and is Australia's oldest lighthouse. There are some excellent cliff-side walks in the area. The Bligh Museum at Adventure Bay has recorded the island's history with the logs of the ships Providence, Bounty and Resolution and a collection of charts, maps and memorabilia.

Mavista Falls

On the slopes of Mount Mangana, off Lockley's Road, is a small reserve with a beautiful small waterfall. A walking track winds through lush growth of stringybark, myrtle and tree ferns.

The Huon Valley

The Huon Highway (A6) follows the Huon River until Surges Bay, where it crosses overland to Dover. It is a lovely drive, with rolling hills and steep green paddocks, and stands of tall gums and pines. The section between Glendevie and Dover is especially picturesque. As you drive along, you can see the striking silhouette of Hartz Peak, looking a bit like Mount Fuji.

Grove

The principal attraction in Grove is the Huon Valley Apple and Heritage Museum. Set in a former packing shed, it has displays of the technology of the apple industry and of 500 different types of apples, with exotic names like Red Limbertwig, Brabant Bellefleur, Roseberry Pippin and Doctor Hogg. It is a reminder of the bustling days before the European Community when Huon Valley apples were keeping the doctor away in the distant British Isles. The museum displays fascinating records for making apple cases, and packing and storing crates. Regular contests were held before World War I. The admission fee includes an apple peeled and cored on the spot with period machinery. Adult $3; children $1.50.

Huonville

South and inland from Snug and Bruny Island is Huonville, the commercial centre of the Channel. It is a pretty area which has pleasant rural and seascape scenery. Along the Huon River early European explorers found valuable softwood for boat building. (Although Huon pine is found in this area, most stands are in the Gordon River area.) The Huon Valley was a large apple exporter before Britain joined the EEC. The population is a little over 1300 people.

Franklin

A small town along the river, with an 1853 pub and several arts and crafts shops, which still has the aura of a Nineteenth Century river port. A good place to browse for antiques.

Geeveston

This timber town is a further 31 km south of Huonville and is a base for visits to the Hartz Mountains National Park and the rugged valleys of the Huon and Picton Rivers. One of the main features in the town is the Esperance Forest & Heritage Centre which combines visitor information, craft displays and forest interpretation. Five forest walks are also available. Adults $$4, children $2.50, families $10.

If you are interested in exploring the forests of southern Tasmania, try the **Tahune Forest Reserve,** about 25 km along the Arve Road from Geeveston. There are a number of lookouts and short walks along the way, with information signs. At the end of the road is the 102 hectare reserve, with picnic facilities on the banks of the Huon River, tall forest and rainforest walks with 1000-year-old Huon pine and 500-year-old celery top pines. Amongst other sights is the Big Tree, a swamp gum 87 metres tall and 21 metres around at the base, and small Huon Pine trailing their branches in the river. At Keogh's Creek there is a level walk through rainforest. Much of this area is logged but carefully managed by Tasmania's Forestry Commission. It is interesting to see how quickly the forest regenerates after being clear-felled.

Dover

From Geeveston the Huon Highway leads south to Dover, a further 21 km. It is the last petrol stop for motorists heading into the lonely and rugged country towards South-East Cape. The Dover Hotel claims to be "Australia's southernmost Hotel Motel". There are two fish processing factories there. It is an important base for the aquaculture industry, with fish farms producing gourmet Atlantic salmon and ocean trout. A picnic spot overlooks the fishing jetties. Southport

Another 21 km south of Dover is the small fishing town and resort of Southport, whose "Southport Settlement" claims to be "Australia's most southern watering hole" with a pub, restaurant and coffee shop. It is the oldest town in the Huon area. Turn left as you enter, away from the beach-front houses and follow the unsealed road to a camping area and white sandy beaches. As you picnic you can look across to Bruny Island and the Southern Ocean.

Nearby is the **Hastings Thermal Pool,** which is 28C all year round. Rain water enters the dolomite area near the caves, descends 600 metres and rises under pressure as a warm spring. **Newdegate Cave** is about 15 minutes' drive away and has beautiful crystalline formations, built up over aeons by calcium saturated water. Its highlight is Titania's Palace, a chamber with a flowstone floor which is rich in straws and stalactites. There are daily tours of the caves, which take about 45 minutes. Adults $10, children 4-18 $5, pensioners $8, family $25.

Lune River is a popular place with gem collectors where you can find fossilised fern, wood agate and crystal. A tramway still operates taking tourists for a 6 km trip through bushland from the township to The Deep Hole across the bay from Southport.

The Derwent Valley and the Central Highlands

For a long one-day trip out of Hobart, explore the lovely Derwent Valley, with its historic towns, opium poppy paddocks, willow-shaded river banks and poplar-lined fields of hops. At the end of the drive along B61 are Mount Field and Lake Pedder and Strathgordon, with their rainforest and knife-edge quartzite mountains. Or, continuing along the Lyell Highway (A10), you find rolling paddocks amidst the encroaching wilderness. Towards the centre are the Central Highlands, with a few scattered hamlets like Bothwell and Waddamana amongst the rivers, lakes and open grazing land.

NEW NORFOLK

As you take the left fork on the A10 towards New Norfolk at Granton, pull up for a few minutes to admire the hundreds of black swans in the Swan Sanctuary.

The next landmark along the road is the Australian Newsprint Mills at Boyer. It was the first in the world to manufacture newsprint from hardwood eucalypt logs. The mill, which produces 240,000 tonnes of paper each year, operates 24 hours a day, every day of the year and produces about 40 per cent of Australia's newsprint.

Nowadays New Norfolk is a town of about 10,000 people about half an hour from Hobart on the banks of the upper Derwent. It is a mixture of quaint old buildings with stately oaks, poplars and pines and ramshackle cottages from the Fifties and Sixties when the Boyer Paper Mill was in its heyday. However it once played an important role in the development of Australia. Not long after the beginning of Van Diemen's Land, the British Government decided that the settlers on Norfolk Island should be relocated, as the isolated island was difficult to provision and the settlers could not support themselves. The first contingent of 34 arrived in 1807, and 544 more within the next year. Although the initial years were hard, New Norfolk's gentle undulating hills and fertile river flats proved ideal for hops.

The immense weatherboard Oast House, one of the most impressive buildings in the town, is the only hop museum in the southern hemisphere. (An oast is a kiln used for drying hops and oast houses are a characteristic feature of the Derwent Valley.) Open every day from 10am, it also has a tea room and an art gallery.

St Matthew's Church of England is the oldest church in Tasmania and one of the most beautiful parish churches in Australia. The original portions of the building date from 1823, but the church was not consecrated until 1825. The lovely stained glass windows and the beautifully carved lectern are particularly interesting.

The Bush Inn was built in 1815 and licensed in 1825, making it the oldest continuously licensed hotel in Australia. Dame Nellie Melba sang here on her last Tasmanian visit in 1927. The Jet Boat departs from the Esplanade at New Norfolk and passengers are taken through shallow, fast-flowing rapids of the Derwent, past the hop fields along the willow-lined river on a brisk 30 minute ride. Rides on the half-hour; bookings at the Bush Inn, 61-3460.

ACCOMMODATION

New Norfolk has abundant accommodation. Here I mention two, with prices for a double room per night, which should be used as a guide only.

Glen Derwent, Lyell Highway, **(03) 6261-3244;**
4 ensuites, double $92-136.

Rosie's Inn, 5 Oast Street, **(03) 6261-1171.**
The old Boyer Hostel now offers pleasant, homey accommodation with 8 ensuites, double B&B $90-120.

Salmon Ponds

About 11 km upriver at Plenty are the famous Salmon Ponds, the oldest trout hatchery in the southern hemisphere. The first trout came here in 1864 after three failed attempts, carefully packed between layers of moss, crushed ice and charcoal, making possible the stocking of many lakes and streams in Australia and New Zealand.

This is a great place for a picnic, with its towering exotic cypresses planted more than 100 years ago. The kids will love it. You can buy a handful of fish food for 20cents to throw it to schools of huge, fat and hungry tiger trout, rainbow trout, brown trout, brook trout, albino trout and Atlantic salmon. The water boils as they race for the pellets. Sometimes a tail smacks the water, drenching an unlucky bystander. There is also a museum with reels, lures and all the paraphernalia of trout fishing and a small restaurant. Open 9am-5pm. Adults $5, children $3, families $14.

Bushy Park

On the way to Mount Field, you pass through the picturesque town of Bushy Park. At one time it was the biggest and most successful hop field in the southern hemisphere. During the summer months there are rows upon rows of hops protected from the wind by rows of poplars fencing the paddocks. In the autumn, the poplars turn yellow, their leaves drift across the road and it looks as if telegraph poles are growing in the hops paddocks. A lovely spot for photography.

Mount Field National Park

Only about 11/2 hours from Hobart, through lovely undulating paddocks, Mount Field is the favourite national park for Hobartians — so famous that it was depicted on a pre-Federation postage stamp! Along with Freycinet, it is the oldest national park in Tasmania. It has a great variety of scenic features and wildlife in its 16,265 hectares and offers a great range of facilities for day visitors. Around the park entrance are picnic facilities and Russell Falls. These cascade in a veil of mist down a cliff face and are surrounded by rain forest. In 1885 a visitor wrote: "How shall I describe this waterfall? Painter and poet together would fail to convey more than a shadow of its sublime grandeur." Hmmm. Well, it's not exactly Niagra Falls, but it's worth a walk down the path which is accessible even by wheelchairs. A bit further afield, the 30-minute Tall Trees Walk over duckboards will take you through a forest that features the world's tallest flowering plant, 85-metre swamp gums. It is great for the children.

If you are a bit more adventurous, drive up the winding unsealed road towards the top of the mountain. About half-way up is the 15-minute Lyrebird Nature Walk which displays the forest in transition from low to high altitudes. At the end of the road is Lake Dobson and an enormous car park — mostly for the crowds who trek here to ski after good snowfalls in the winter. The one-hour Pandani Grove Walk skirts the edges of Lake Dobson and passes through groves of ancient pencil pine and tall pandani.

There are some wonderful day walks to other tarns in the area gouged out by ancient glaciers. The combination of the stark beauty of the lichened rock, exotic plants like pencil pine and fagus, and the mountain ridge towering overhead, make hiking

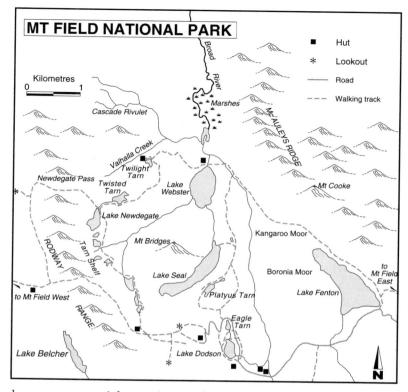

here a very special experience. The views from the top of Mount Field are superb.

There are a number of well-marked trails to Mount Field West, South West Lookout, Platypus Tarn, Lake Fenton, Lake Seal and other destinations, but they all require a bit of preparation. The weather at Mount Field changes by the day and sometimes by the hour. Snowfalls can occur in the high country at any time of the year. The Parks and Wildlife Service recommends that you take clothing for all types of weather. A waterproof jacket with a hood is essential. Always take a haversack with spare clothing and food.

Ouse

This unremarkable little town (pronounced "ooze") has a very attractive convict-built Anglican Church dedicated to St John the Baptist (1843), with five lovely stained glass windows and skilful wood carving. The old cemetery is worth strolling through.

Hamilton

In 1844 Hamilton was a bustling town with two breweries, six or seven inns, stone quarries and three agricultural implement makers. It was marked down as a major country centre with squares, an esplanade, a circus and municipal reserve. But after a burst in convict days, its population peaked at 400 in 1881, and it gradually decayed. Today, it is a quiet hamlet full of charming historic sandstone buildings. It is well worth a stroll and a quiet picnic in the park next to the Clyde River.

The Anglican Church of St Peters is one of Australia's oldest (1834) and was built before Melbourne was founded. It has only one door, a detail attributed to the desire to keep convicts from absconding during services. It has four interesting stained glass windows, but its most memorable feature is a terse inscription on a memorial plaque to Privates William John Alder Brown and Harold Baylie Brown of the AIF, both killed in Gallipoli on 2 May 1915, sons of W.C. Brown, the Council Clerk, and C.A. Brown. It brings alive the pain of what was once called "the Great War".

Bothwell

You can reach Bothwell from the Midlands Highway through A5 or from the Lyell Highway through B110. It is so far off the beaten track that time has passed it by, making it a treasure house of Australia's colonial heritage. Most buildings here were built with convict labour and feature explanatory plaques which can be examined on a leisurely walk. The early settlers were Scottish and they brought with them a passion for golf. Ratho, a nine-hole private course not far from the centre of town, is Australia's first. The exact date is a matter of some dispute but it was played on some time before 1840. The fairways are kept short by grazing sheep on them and the greens are surrounded by fences to preserve the putting surface. If you hit a fence, you are allowed another shot without penalty. A golf museum is now housed in the old schoolhouse.

Bothwell's attractions include the War Memorial Sundial, the only one of its kind in the Southern Hemisphere. The Anglican Church of St Michael and All Angels (1891) is one of only two churches in Australia with an open fireplace. It is an imposing place of worship with the circular staircase leading to the belfry, carved lecterns, an Italian mosaic of the Risen Christ, and high altar of sandstone. The plainer Presbyterian Church of St Luke, designed by John Lee Archer and built in 1831, stands like a sentinel at the top of Alexander Street. Archer's original design called for rounded windows, but Lieutenant-Governor Arthur directed him to change them, as he considered the design "unchristian". Some of the best trout fishing in the Southern Hemisphere takes place not far from Bothwell.

Waddamana

Less than an hour from Bothwell, towards the northwest, is Waddamana, a retired power station that has become a popular tourist attraction. This was the first major hydro-electric development in Tasmania. Opened in 1916, it provided only seven megawatts of electricity — but enough for the 1999 subscribers in Hobart. (Waddamana "B", the new power station, can generate about seven times that amount.) The exhibits give a fascinating glimpse of the adventure of civil and power engineering that make modern life possible.

The Midlands

A rich farming and grazing area, the Midlands was one of the first regions settled in Tasmania. Many of the little towns off the Heritage Highway from Hobart to Launceston are of great historic interest. Time has passed most of them by and they now have a quaint period character. You will find what is probably the largest collection of Georgian architecture and colonial buildings in Australia.

Bridgewater

This town is close enough to be counted as an outer suburb of Hobart. It is the location of the main north-south crossing of the Derwent River. The Causeway across the river was constructed in the early 1830s by 200 convicts in chains who wheelbarrowed in two million tons of stone and clay. The first bridge was opened in 1849; today's bridge dates from 1946. Brighton and Pontville

Just beyond Bridgewater are the adjoining towns of Brighton and Pontville. Since 1826, Brighton has been the home of Brighton Army Camp, which was the main military post in Tasmania. More recently it was used to house refugees from the war in Kosovo. Pontville dates from 1830. St Mark's Church of England is an imposing and attractive parish church with an interesting cemetery surrounding it. St Matthew's Catholic Church is one of the most attractive in Hobart.

Kempton

First settled in the 1820s, Kempton had Tasmania's first market-place for stock and produce. Other industries of the day included a flour mill and a brewery. Numerous hotels and lodging houses catered for weary travellers along the highway. Many of the buildings can be seen today. The present St Mary's Church dates back to 1841. The Congregational Church is one year older. There are many other fine Victorian and Georgian buildings, including the restored Wilmot Arms Inn (1844). At the Council Chambers you can get a copy of "Historic Township of Kempton".

Oatlands

Once mooted as the State capital, Oatlands has about 140 original Georgian sandstone buildings — the largest collection in a village in Australia — and it still retains the atmosphere of a Nineteenth Century country town. It was established as a military garrison in 1827 to guard settlers from marauding Aborigines. St Peter's Church of England was designed in part by John Lee Archer. St Paul's, the neo-Gothic Catholic church is an architectural treasure. It was built as a small medieval village church according to a design by Augustus Pugin, the English architect who created all the decorative detail in the Houses of Parliament in London. He took a great interest in Tasmania and had a hand in several Catholic churches here.

The two-storey sandstone Callington Mill is one of the most photographed buildings in Tasmania and a symbol of the Midlands region. It is said to be the only surviving structure of its kind in Tasmania. For a $2 admission fee, you can pay a visit to the grounds. Someday, it is hoped, the sails will be restored. Behind the mill is a mysterious depression with a forested sandstone island like a plug in the middle. This is Lake Dulverton, which has been dry since 1993, although there are plans to fill it again.

Ross

The town of Ross lies exactly on the 42nd parallel and is probably the most picturesque of the towns along the Midland Highway, with charming colonial building and the leafy elms lining its streets. Peering into the back yard of the local homes you can see sandstone sheds and you feel as if you have been transported back 120 years.

The best-known feature in Ross is the 1836 sandstone bridge. Constructed on the orders of Governor Arthur and designed by John Lee Archer, it was constructed by two convicts, Daniel Herbert and James Colbeck, who later received pardons as a reward for their work. The arches contain 184 stones depicting Celtic symbols interspersed with images of notable personalities and carvings of animals.

With many other buildings from the colonial era, Ross has been classified by the National Trust. In the heart of the town is an intersection with buildings on each of the four corners which the locals are said to call "Temptation", the Man O'Ross Hotel; "Salvation", the Catholic church; "Recreation", the town hall; and "Damnation", the former gaol. The tourist information centre is located in the tearooms, which were originally St John's Anglican Church. There are many interesting buildings in the village — 1836 War Memorial, Sherwood Castle Inn, Macquarie Store and the Old Barracks Building (now a wool craft centre). The local Uniting Church at the top of the main street, opened in 1885, has blackwood pews, two fine stained glass windows and a modern Aubusson tapestry.

Not far away from the church is the site of a "female factory" where up to 600 convict women and their babies were imprisoned between 1848 and 1854. The women were trained as domestics and then hired out to surrounding properties or worked in the central laundry. Nowadays, it is just ruins, but the restored overseer's cottage gives some idea of what life was like under those circumstances.

Local properties consistently obtain record prices for their superfine wool and the history of the nation's wool industry is well documented in the Tasmanian Wool Centre (03) 6381-5466. Adults $4, children $2, family $10.

Northeastern Tasmania

The North-east region forms an enormous triangle north from Hobart to Launceston and east to St Helens, a landmark for anyone flying from the Mainland to Hobart. (We have assumed that you will be travelling north from Hobart.) The principal tourist attractions are along the winding roads of the coast, although there are some fascinating old mining towns and excellent bush-walking inland. The Sun Coast, Tasmania's favourite holiday spot, has sheltered beaches, rocky coastline, terrific surf and great fishing.

Buckland

After leaving Hobart, drive past Hobart airport, to Sorell, then follow the A3 highway to Buckland and Orford. Buckland is a small country town sprawling on either side of the highway whose main attraction is a handsome stone Anglican parish church dedicated to St John the Baptist, built in 1846. Surrounding the church yard is a stone wall and scattered around it are a number of graves shaded by sombre cedars. It looks as if a bit of England had been transported to this distant pocket of Van Diemen's Land. And, in fact, the fame of the Church is due to its beautiful East window in the sanctuary, with three panels representing John in the desert, the baptism of Christ and John's beheading, all in brilliant colours. As improbable as it may seem, the window, done in a style known as "white grisaille", apparently dates to between 1350 and 1400. It is well worth a quick visit.

Orford

Once an important port, Orford is now a popular holiday resort and fishing village. There are many interesting walks in the area. The town boasts at least 8 decent motels/villas, a youth convention centre, and a caravan park. About 6 km south of Orford is the Thumbs Lookout, 550 metres above sea level with spectacular views of the Mercury Passage and Maria Island. If you are using Orford as a base for an exploration of the area, you might take in the Sandspit Forest Reserve, which has a 20-hectare stand of relict rainforest. It is a survivor from an era thousands of years ago when the climate on the East Coast was much wetter and favoured rainforest. This has survived because it lies in a damp protected gully which has been untouched by fire for the past 5000 years. A 20-minute, duck-boarded walkway has been constructed to show what a rainforest is.

Triabunna

Triabunna, the destination of many of the log trucks that thunder along the highway, is a commercial port that houses the APPM woodchip mill. The Pioneer and Working Horse Museum is a popular attraction, with shearing, blacksmithing and Clydesdales.

Maria Island National Park

This popular park lies 15 km off the coast and 88 km north-east of Hobart. It can be reached by a 50-passenger catamaran ferry from the Eastcoaster Resort, which lies between Orford and Triabunna. Weather permitting, the catamaran makes three runs at 10.30am, 1.30pm and 3.30pm daily throughout the year with an extra trip at 9am in the summer holidays. For bookings and confirmation of the timetable, contact Eastcoaster Express, **(03) 6257-1172.** Day trips: adults $17, children U14 $10. Campers:

Settler's Cottage, Maria Island

adults $20, children U14 $13. You disembark at Darlington, an abandoned town. The island is unique amongst Australia's national parks, with both spectacular scenery and a fascinating history. Maria Island was actually the first penal colony established in Tasmania, in 1825. By 1828 there were 145 convicts, but due to the success of Port Arthur, the settlement was abolished in 1832. After another ten years, a convict probation station was established at Darlington. Five New Zealand Maoris were imprisoned from 1846 for "open rebellion against the Queen". One died there and in 1988 his body was exhumed and taken back to New Zealand. After the prison era, an Italian entrepreneur set up first a wine-making and silk industry and then a cement works, all of which eventually failed.

Maria Island is well-known for its abundant animal life. It is the only national park in Tasmania where all 11 of the state's endemic bird species can be observed. The endangered *Cape Barren goose* has thrived here, along with the forty-spotted pardalote. There are a number of fascinating walks, and the local limestone is studded with fossils. Facilities on Maria Island are basic. There are no shops. Limited hostel accommodation is available in the Penitentiary Units (your chance to sleep in a prison). These are often booked six months in advance ($8 per person). There is a camping ground for $6-8 per person.

SWANSEA

Situated 137 km from Hobart and 51km north of Triabunna, Swansea has abundant accommodation and is ideally suited for a beach holiday or as a base for exploring Maria Island. Take a stroll around the town. The All Saints Anglican Church on Noyes Street is a lovely example of late Victorian stonework. There is a cemetery overlooking Great Oyster Bay with an interesting grave — the six children of an emigrant family named Large, who drowned in 1850 just before they disembarked to take up a new life in Swansea. The parents were saved, but returned to Hobart.

ACCOMMODATION

Schouten House, 1 Waterloo Road, **(03) 6257-8177,**
4 ensuites, double B&B $126. Schouten House also has a superb restaurant with great Italian fare and seafood.

Meredith House, 15 Noyes Street, **(03) 6257-8119,**
11 ensuites, double B&B $124-144.

Swansea Motor Inn, 1 Franklin Street, **(03) 6257-8102,**
35 ensuites, double $50-90.

Scarecrow Cottage, 22 Noyes Street, **0408-491-958;**
1 ensuite, double B&B $125.

Swansea Caravan Park, Shaw Street, **(03) 6257-8177;**
9 cabins, double $25-35. Linen extra.

THE FREYCINET PENINSULA AND COLES BAY

The Freycinet Peninsula (pronounced Fray-sin-nay) is a place of captivating pink granite cliffs, dazzling blue seas and long white sandy beaches. It is now the most popular national park in Tasmania. (The Tasmanian poet James McAuley wrote a whole book of poems about the area.) Much of the park is coastal heathland with brilliant wildflowers in the spring. There are large shell middens in the park, relics of its long occupation by Aborigines of the Oyster Bay tribe. Moulting Bay Lagoon is a wetland of international importance with many black swans. Two or three-hour easy bushwalks are well worthwhile. The road south ends at a car park from which you can climb 20 minutes to a lookout over Wineglass Bay, one of the most photographed spots in the State, with an unspoilt white beach stretching in a perfect curve along the clear blue water. A three-hour walk to the top of Mt Amos gives some spectacular views.

For the really adventurous, try Schouten Island, a seldom-visited section of the national park, just off the tip of the peninsula. There is no jetty, but the walks are very interesting — a true desert island.

Nearby Coles Bay has accommodation for tours of the Freycinet Peninsula. Demand is very high during the holiday season and we advise you to book ahead. To get to Coles Bay you have to travel about 30 km north from Swansea before turning south onto 30 km of partly dirt road.

ACCOMMODATION

Freycinet Lodge, in the National Park, **(03) 6257-0101,** 60 ensuites, double $150.

Cottages By The Sea, Coles Bay Road, Hepburn Point, **(03) 6257-0102,** 11 ensuites, double $120-168.

Iluka Holiday Centre, Muirs Beach, **(03) 6257-0115.** Ensuite double $50-90; caravan double $40, hostel dormitory single $13-16.

BICHENO

The town of Bicheno is 43 km north of Swansea, and is an artist's and photographer's paradise. The beaches are covered in an incredibly soft silver sand that is unique to the area. Off the main beach is Diamond Island, home to the fairy penguin, and it is possible to walk out to it at low tide. Keep an eye on the time and tide because the behaviour of the penguins can be very absorbing, and you may find that you have to swim back to the beach.

Bicheno entered history as a whaling station, and is now a popular fishing and boating spot. The grave of an Aboriginal woman named Waubededar who lived with the sealers is visited by many tourists. There is a sea life centre, and bird and animal parks nearby. The surfing off Cape Lodt is usually very good.

EATING OUT

Many of the larger hotels and motels have good eating places.

Waub's Bay House, 16 Tasman Highway, **(03) 6375-1193.**
Probably the best in Bicheno. Sensibly priced and delicious seafood. Licensed.

Sea Life Centre Restaurant, 1 Tasman Highway, **(03) 6375-1121.**
On the waterfront, with the best views in town. Seafood is their specialty. Licensed.

Bicheno Beachfront, Tasman Highway, **(03) 6375-1111.**
Good counter meals and restaurant fare for the family. Silver Sands,

Burgess Street, **(03) 6375-1266.**
Good restaurant and counter meals for the family.

ACCOMMODATION

Accommodation here is ample because the town is a popular resort in the summer.

Bicheno Holiday Village, The Esplanade, **(03) 6375-1171,** 20 ensuites, double $110-135.

Silver Sands Resort Hotel, Burgess Street, **(03) 6375-1266,** 35 ensuites, double $50-75.

Bicheno Cabin and Tourist Park, 4 Champ Street, **1300-302-075.** 15 ensuites, double $50-68; caravan double $30-40.

Douglas-Aspley National Park

North of Bicheno are the forested hills and river gorges of the Douglas-Aspley region. Its hallmark, the dramatic dolerite spire of Nichols Cap, is visible from the Tasman Highway. It takes in Tasmania's largest remaining area of dry sclerophyll forest, as well as waterfalls, gorges, lookouts and two rivers. The waters of the Douglas River are home to the *Southern Grayling,* one of Australia's rarest fish, and the park's ecological diversity of wildlife and plant life is remarkable. A walk into the Aspley waterhole takes only 10 minutes. A return trip to the Aspley Gorge takes three hours.

Fingal

Inland from St Marys is the Fingal district, best-known for the World Coal Shovelling Championships held there each March, which attract thousands of spectators. Many of the small townships in the area flourished and faded with the rise and decline of coal mining. The three churches in Fingal, built between 1861 and 1881, contain some of the state's finest traditional window leadlighting. At nearby Mangana the Catholic church is a gem, with nearly everything designed in Edwardian style by a well-known Launceston architect - a reminder of past prosperity.

North of Fingal, off B43, are some interesting forest reserves. Forestry is now one of the main sources of employment in the area after local mines ceased operation. The Mathinna Falls is a four-tier waterfall which drops over 80 metres. An easy 30-minute return walk leads to the base of the falls. To the east of Mathinna is the Evercreech Forest Reserve which contains the "White Knights", the tallest white gums in the world — 300 years old and 89 metres high. A gentle 20-minute walk has interpretive signs to help visitors understand why these trees were able to grow so tall.

SCAMANDER

Situated at the mouth of the Scamander River, this town has spectacular ocean beaches. Mainly a resort town, it has some first-class accommodation and a large resort with excellent dining facilities. Here is a selection.

ACCOMMODATION

Scamander Beach Resort Hotel, Tasman Highway, **(03) 6372-5255,**
57 ensuites, pool, sauna, playground, double $60-75.

Pelican Sands, Tasman Highway, **(03) 6372-5231,**
18 ensuites, pool, double $55-75.

Kookaburra Caravan and Camping Ground, Tasman Highway, **(03) 6372-5121,**
caravan double $25, linen extra.

ST HELENS

This resort town is on Georges Bay, a further 37 km north. It is a popular holiday and commercial fishing centre, and the most northern town on the east coast. From here the road swings westward towards Scottsdale through some beautiful mountain country. The permanent population of St Helens is 1000 but this swells during the summer. The History Room at St Helens has photographs and memorabilia displaying the maritime and mining history of the region. It is a treasure trove of information about places to visit in the area. Admission: adults $4, children $2, family $12.

For those interested in bushwalking while holidaying at St Helens, the Blue Tier is a must. About 45 minutes to the west, turn north to Goulds Country, an all-timber village classified by the National Trust. It is a bit difficult to find, but you can get directions from the History Room. The Blue Tier is a mountain plateau which was once the site of a hectic tin mining industry. Apart from some panoramic views and noteworthy vegetation, there are many ruins of mines and houses. Some of the walks are duckboarded. Around St Helens are Humbug Point State Recreation Area, St Helens Point State Recreation Area and the Bay of Fires Coastal Reserve. Here you can take a number of scenic walks along some of the State's most beautiful beaches. There are huge sand dunes at St Helens Point with Aboriginal middens.

EATING OUT

Tidal Water Restaurant, cnr Tasman Highway and Jason Street, **(03) 6376-1100.** Up-market modern Australian cooking, with excellent seafood.

Anchor Wheel Restaurant, 59-61 Tully Street, **(03) 6376-1358.** Hearty family fare at reasonable prices. Bayside Inn, 2 Cecilia Street, (03) 6376-1466. Famed for their seafood chowder.

Wok Stop, Cecilia Street, **(03) 6376-2665.** Lovely Chinese dining, with takeaways available as well.

ACCOMMODATION

Prices of accommodation in St Helens vary considerably depending on the standard and the season. Here we have a selection, with prices for a double room per night, which should be used as a guide only.

Warrawee Guest House, Tasman Highway, **(03) 6376-1987,**
6 ensuites, double B&B $92-130.

Artnor Lodge, 71 Cecilia Street, **(03) 6376-1234,**
6 ensuites, barbecue, playground, double $60-68.

St Helens Bayside Inn, 2 Cecilia Street, **(03) 6376-1466,**
54 ensuites, licensed restaurant, heated pool, double $47-81.

St Helens Caravan Park, Penelope Street, **(03) 6376-1290,**
caravan double $30-35, cabin double $40-55.

St Helens Youth Hostel, 5 Cameron Street, **(03) 6376-1661,**
22 guests in 4 dorms, dining room, double $26-32.

Mount William National Park

This national park was proclaimed in 1973 for the conservation of the *Forester Kangaroo,* now restricted to several small areas of the state. They can be seen throughout the park. From Mount William there are breathtaking views all the way to the Furneaux group of islands in Bass Strait. It was over a land bridge formed in part by these islands that the Aborigines first came to Tasmania and one of the park's features is huge middens. A spectacular example is at Musselroe Point. The Eddystone Point lighthouse is a local landmark. There are two access roads. The northern end can be reached by following the signs from Gladstone; the ranger's office is 17 km along a gravel road. The southern end of the park can be reached from St Helens, via Ansons Bay road. It is about 50 km from St Helens to Eddystone Point along a gravel road.

Weldborough

For history buffs, the Chinese burial plot in the little town of Weldborough is worth visiting. Chinese first arrived in Tasmania from Canton in about 1870 to work in the tin mines. They once outnumbered Europeans in the area, but the last of the once-flourishing community died in 1994. The town once had its own joss house and Chinese casino and in the surrounding bush are many Chinese artefacts.

Derby

More history can be found in Derby in the Derby Tin Mine Centre, with a museum display of machinery, photographs and gemstones that chronicles the rise and fall of the area as a centre for alluvial tin mining. A mining shanty town has been recreated in the gardens surrounding the museum. Have a go at panning for tin! Adults $4, children $1.50, family $10.

Scottsdale

Scottsdale, with a population around 5000, is 70 km north-east of Launceston, and is the centre of a large market garden area. A food processing factory specialising in deep freezing and dehydrating vegetables is located here. Oil poppies are grown in the area, and when they bloom in January and February the countryside is a blaze of colour. Lavender is grown around Nabowla, 13 km west of Scottsdale. It blooms in late December through January and the air is filled with its perfume. One local landmark is the Sideling, a 577 metre hill which gives a magnificent panoramic view as far as the northern coastline and the Bass Strait. The Scottsdale area also contains some of the best timber in Tasmania. Many of the giant blue gums milled here were used for piling the Suez Canal and several great English ports.

BRIDPORT

On the coast about 20 km from Scottsdale is the district's playground, Bridport, with several attractive and safe beaches for both bathers and water skiers. A good place to stay and take your time enjoying the district.

One of the local attractions is the Bridestowe Estate Lavender Farm, Golconda Road, Nabowla, **(03) 6352-8182.** This is one of the world's largest properties for producing flower oil for the perfume industry and a very popular tourist spot, with its endless purple paddocks of fragrant lavender. It is open to visitors during the flowering season, from mid-December until the end of January. Adults $3, children U16 free.

ACCOMMODATION

Bridport Motor Inn, 105 Main Street, **(03) 6356-1238,** 4 ensuites, licensed bistro, double $70-75.

Bridairre, Frances Street, **(03) 6356-1438.**

Launceston

Launceston is Australia's largest inland port, and Tasmania's second largest city with about 94,000 people. It is situated at the head of the Tamar River at the junction of the north and south Esk, in the central northern region of Tasmania. In the summer the temperature ranges between 21C and 13C and in the winter between 13C and 5C. The average rainfall is approximately 750mm with the wettest period from May to October.

The fortunes of Launceston have declined a bit since its heyday in the late Nineteenth Century. At that time it was a very progressive city — in 1847 it saw the first use of anaesthetic in the Southern Hemisphere and in 1895 it became the first city in Australia with electric lighting. Today it still gives the impression of modest prosperity: a garden city with many well established beautiful public parks and private gardens. Wood-frame houses sprawl over the steep hills which overlook the highway and the factories and shops of the commercial district. The buildings have a distinctively Victorian flavour with many architectural gems. Geographically, its most striking feature is the Cataract Gorge Reserve, a piece of wilderness just 15 minutes' walk from the city centre. In the hinterland is rich agricultural country with wineries, orchards and farms producing famed Tasmanian wools, foods and wines.

There is an intense rivalry between Hobart and Launceston, perhaps owing to the fact that "Launie", as most Tasmanians call it, is the oldest city in Australia after Sydney and Hobart. "You know the best thing about Hobart?", petrol station attendants quip. "It's the road going north." ABC Radio once received a complaint that sportsmen from Launceston were described by Hobart comperes as coming from Tasmania when they played well, and from Launceston when they behaved badly.

HOW TO GET THERE

By air
Qantas/Southern Airlines and Ansett fly to/from Melbourne, Sydney, Brisbane and the Gold Coast. The single for the airport shuttle is $10. Taxis to the City cost about $20.

By sea
The Spirit of Tasmania passenger and car ferry operates between Melbourne and Devonport. The coach fare from Devonport to Launceston is about $14. The Devil Cat passenger and vehicle catamaran operates between Melbourne and George Town, north of Launceston. The coach fare to the City is about $10.

By bus
Redline Coaches operate a Hobart/Launceston and Launceston/Devonport, Burnie, Wynyard and Smithton service. For bushwalkers, TWT Tassielink offers services to Cradle Mountain and Lake St Clair, (03) 6334-4442. Their depot is at 101 George Street.

By road
The trip from Hobart is 200 km, via the Midlands Highway and takes approximately 2.5 hours. From Burnie, 150 km away, it takes about the same time. From the east coast (St. Helens), via Scottsdale, the 165 km trip is again about 21/2 hours. Tourist information
   The Tasmanian Visitor Information Centre, at the corner of St John and Paterson Streets, is open Monday to Friday 9am-5pm, Saturday 9am-4pm and Sunday 9am-noon, (03) 6336-3133.

LAUNCESTON

0   100   200 km

Lindsay

Goderich Street

Street

RIVER

ESK

Esplanade

Tamar

Street

NORTH

Street

City Park

Shields St

George

William

St John

Street

Street

Brisbane

Street

Windmill Hill
Reserve

Charles

Cimitiere

Town
Hall

GPO

Street

Earl St

York

Royal
Park

Police

Civic Square

Information

Welman

Cameron

Street

Street

Queen Victoria
Museum

Wellington

Mall

Street

Street

George

Street

Kings
Park

Paterson

Street

Street

Brisbane

Bathurst

Street

Street

Princes
Square

St John

Street

Street

ny Royal
World

York

Elizabeth

Wellington

Charles

Street

Street

Bourke

Margaret

Frederick

Batten Street

King Street

Sheppy St

James St

Thomas St.

Edmund St.

Street

Street

Brickfields
Reserve

Street

Canning

1

Arbour
Park

Hillside Cres

Upton

Alice Place

Rocher St.

Balfour

Crown Street

Frankland

Street

Hospital

Hospital

Street

Street

Ockerby
Gardens

Howick

ACCOMMODATION

Launceston has plenty of accommodation, from five-star to budget. Here we have a selection, with prices for a double room per night. Use it only as a guide

Country Club Casino, Prospect Vale, **1800-030-211,**
104 ensuites, licensed restaurant, bistro, heated indoor pool, spa, sauna, tennis, squash, golf; double $225-395.

Colonial Motor Inn, cnr George and Elizabeth Streets,
(03) 6331-6588,
64 ensuites, double $120-195.

Prince Albert Inn, William & Tamar Streets, **1800 632 351,**
12 rooms, and elegant old world style hotel, breakfast included, double $120-$180.

Archer's Manor, 17 Alanvale Road, **(03) 6326-3600,**
34 ensuites, licensed restaurant, double $70-125.

Kilmarnock House, 66 Elphin Road, **(03) 6334 1514,**
10 apartments with ensuite, kitchenette, self contained, good value B&B, double $90-$110.

Edenholme Grange, 14 St Andrew's Street, **(03) 6334 6666,**
21 rooms, 4 with ensuite, 2 apartments, a delightful bed and breakfast in a victorian manor set in grounds on the edge of the city, double $110-$138.

Brickfield Terrace, 64 and 68 Margaret Street, **ph 1 800 632 351,**
10 suites including 2 apartments, two storeyed terraces with all the amenities - homey feel, kids welcome, B&B, double $135-$140.

Highfield House, 23 Welham Street, ph **(03) 6334 3485,**
5 rooms with ensuite, breakfast room classic victorian residence - double $126.

Abel Tasman Airport Motor Inn, 303 Hobart Road, Kings Meadow, **(03) 6344-5244,**
42 ensuites, licensed restaurant, double B&B $80.

Treasure Island Caravan Park, 94 Glen Dhu Street, South Launceston, **(03) 6344-2600,**
22 units, double $54-60.

Launceston Youth Hostel, 36 Thistle Street, **(03) 6344-9779,**
13 dormitories, single $12.

EATING OUT

Launceston has some excellent restaurants. Most are BYO and those that are licensed have a corkage charge if you bring your own.

Shrimps, 72 George Street, **(03) 6334-0584.**
Excellent seafood is the house specialty.
Quigleys, 96 Balfour Street, **(03) 6331-6971.**
Very popular for its French cuisine, licensed.
Cafe Gazebo, 135 George Street, **(03) 6331-0110.**
Top flight dining for a quiet night out.
Calabrisella, 56 Wellington Street, **(03) 6331-1958.**
Good-value and very tasty Italian fare.
Elm Cottage, 168 George Street, **(03) 6331-8468.**
Atmospheric dining for a pleasant night out.
Satay House, Kings Court Shopping Centre, Kings Meadow, **(03) 6344-5955.**
Indonesian meals.

ENTERTAINMENT

There are several lively spots to have a drink.

The Star Bar Cafe, 113 Charles Street, **31-9659,** recently refurbished in a continental style. It offers coffees, pizzas and delicious Mississippi mudcake. It was the 1994 best Australian Bistro.

Irish Murphy's, cnr Bathurst and Brisbane Streets. Live entertainment with an Irish flavour.

The Metz, cnr St John and York Streets. Varied entertainment.

The Royal Oak, cnr Brisbane and Tamar Streets, **31-5346,** is the popular watering hole for the country set.

The Saloon Bar at Hotel Tasmania, 191 Charles Street, **31-7355.** Wild West dcor; a popular spot to have a drink.

SIGHTSEEING

The Cataract Gorge is a spectacular asset for city life and it is only a few minutes by bus from the centre. A 1.5 kilometre walk along the face of the cliff ends in the Cataract Cliff Grounds Reserve from which a chairlift with the longest single span in the world crosses the gorge. The lift's total length is 457 metres and its central span is 308 metres. Manicured gardens, complete with strutting peacocks, merge with native flora on the upper bank, while on the city side, gardens surrounding a swimming pool extend to the lake over which you pass in the chairlift. The river water is deep, cold and dangerous and too cold to swim in. Signs are posted with dire warnings about hypothermia.

There are many quaint malls and shopping centres in the city such as the Quadrant Mall and Yorktown Square. The Queen Victoria Museum and Art Gallery in Wellington Street is a fascinating place to visit. It has a unique collection of Tasmanian fauna and Aboriginal artefacts, one of Australia's finest collections of colonial paintings, and a reconstructed joss-house which gives an insight into Australia's Chinese heritage. Open Mon-Sat, 10am-5pm, Sun 2pm-5pm. Admission free.

Launceston Planetarium is one of four planetariums in Australia. From Tues-Sat half-hour shows commence at 2pm and 3pm. Admission to the Planetarium: adult $3; children $2; family $7. NB: children under 5 are not admitted to the public shows.

The Umbrella Shop, in George Street, is built entirely of Tasmanian Blackwood and is preserved by the National Trust as the last genuine period shop in Tasmania.

The City Park was first established in the 1820s. It is spacious with well laid-out gardens amid old elm and oak trees. It contains a small zoo and houses the John Hart Conservatory which is noted for its displays of begonias, cyclamen and many other hot house blooms. A very pleasant place for picnics.

The Penny Royal World, in Paterson Street, is an imaginative man-made development. It depicts early Nineteenth Century gunpowder mills, cannon foundry and arsenal in an old four-acre quarry with streams and waterfalls. Within the complex there is a canal system and lake complete with a fleet of vessels, two of which fire and proof their guns daily. A scale model railway system runs the 700 metres from the Gunpowder Mill to the Penny Royal Watermill complex. Admission: family $49.50 (2 adults and 6 children); adult $19.50; children $9.50.

The Country Club Casino at Prospect Vale, besides accommodation mentioned above, has various gaming tables and offers live entertainment.

Franklin House, 7 km south, is an early settler's home furnished in the colonial style and built in 1838. It is owned by the National Trust - open for inspection daily 9am-12.30pm, 1.30pm-5pm. Admission $4.

Outlying attractions

In Launceston many tours, both half day and full day, and a variety of travel packages, are offered to see the sights of the Tamar Valley and the area surrounding Launceston. For details, contact the Tasmanian Visitor Information Centre, (03) 6336-3122.

TRAVELLING SOUTH

Longford

About 10 km off the Midlands Highway is Longford. First settled in 1813, it still retains the charm of a bygone era. Two of the best-known attractions are two well-reserved colonial homes, Woolmers Estate and Brickendon Historic Farm.

Evandale

Best known nowadays for the National Penny Farthing Championships, Evandale is an historic town with beautifully preserved colonial buildings only 15 minutes away from Launceston. St Andrew's Uniting Church must be unique, with its Roman temple facade and a statue of a noble Roman watching over the gravestones scattered throughout the churchyard. Every Sunday Evandale is also the site of Tasmania's biggest country market.

The area is rich in historical associations. The father of the bushranger Ned Kelly served time as a prisoner here; John Batman arrested bushranger Martin Cash nearby in 1826; artist John Glover executed some of his paintings here. Glover's house, Clarendon, is now administered by the National Trust. It is situated on the banks of the South Esk and has extensive formal gardens and beautiful parklands. It is open daily from 10am-5pm. Adults $6, family $12.

Ben Lomond

Evandale is also the gateway to Ben Lomond National Park. With its steep cliffs Ben Lomond is visible over much of the northern midlands. In the winter it has the best ski fields in the State, although it must be admitted that they will never rival Aspen or even Thredbo. Its facilities include excellent downhill and cross country runs, a ski school with instructors, skis, clothing and toboggan hire, a ski patrol, chain hire and tows. There are bus services from most major centres. In the summer, its craggy heights offer plenty of opportunities for bushwalking, abseiling and rock climbing. The plateau is roughly 14 km in length and 6 km in width and more than 1300 metres high. Legges Tor on the plateau is the second highest point in Tasmania (1572 metres). It is an excellent place to observe the vegetation of the exposed

mountain tops. The dolerite columns and scree slopes will interest geologists. The park is about an hour's drive from Launceston and three hours from Hobart. The road to the plateau is unsealed and the final section climbs Jacobs Ladder, a steep drive with six hairpin bends, almost vertical drops and no safety barriers. Wheel chains must be carried between June and September.

Liffey Falls

Around 60 km south-west via Carrick and Bracknell, are the Liffey Falls. It is a popular destination for bushwalkers and fishermen. There is a large fernery here which sells a great variety of ferns. The falls are in a reserve and drop into a beautiful rainforest.

TRAVELLING NORTH

Exeter

Situated 24 km to the north-west along the Tamar River, Exeter is the centre of a fruit growing area, and even the local school has its own farm. At the mouth of the Supply River are the remains of Tasmania's first water-driven flour mill.

Batman Bridge

The bridge spans the Tamar River another 30 km downstream at Whirlpool Reach. It was one of the world's first cable-stayed bridges. Dominated by a 100 metre high steel A-frame inclined 20 degrees from the vertical, it leans out 30 metres across the river and carries almost the entire weight of the 206 metre main span. The bridge was opened in 1968.

Bell Bay

Further downstream and very close to the coast, Bell Bay has become an important inland port mainly nourished by Comalco's aluminium smelter and Tempco's manganese steel furnaces. The Hydro-Electric Commission runs a thermal generating plant here to supplement its hydro generating capacity.

George Town

The town is the residential and commercial centre for Bell Bay, but offers little in the way of accommodation. It was one of the earliest settlements in Australia. It has a beautiful Georgian mansion, *The Grove*, that has been restored and is open for inspection daily 10am-5pm; admission $2.50.

Low Head

Just 5 km north of George Town is Australia's oldest continuously running pilot station, the Low Head Pilot Station. The building itself was erected in 1835 and now houses the Maritime Museum. Low Head is also a popular holiday resort and picnic area.

Beaconsfield

Now a quiet country town, Beaconsfield became a thriving mining centre when gold was discovered there in 1869. The ruins of brick buildings with Romanesque arches at an old pithead are a reminder of its exciting past. The mine was closed in 1914 because of water seepage. The Grub Shaft Gold Mine and Heritage Museum displays a fascinating collection of local memorabilia.

Asbestos Range National Park

Established in 1976, this park is teeming with wildlife and is an important grazing ground for the endangered *Forester Kangaroo*. You can also find sandy beaches, flowering heath and splendid views to the Western Tiers. Asbestos was once mined at the park's southern end near Beaconsfield.

TRAVELLING WEST

Trevallyn State Recreation Area

Five kilometres from the centre of Launceston is Lake Trevallyn, which was formed by the damming of the South Esk waters for hydro-electric power in 1955. This dam replaced the Duck Reach power station further downstream which was Tasmania's first hydro-electric power station, built in 1895. The park is a pleasant place for a picnic.

Hadspen

Located some 13 km south-west, the village of Hadspen may bring back memories of the English countryside. Entally House is the most historic of the National Trust properties. It is believed to have been built in 1819 by the eldest son of Mary Reiby of Sydney. It has a fine collection of Regency furniture and silver. Set in superb grounds and gardens, Entally has a green house, chapel and coach house. It is open daily 10am-12.30pm and 1-5pm. Adults $6, family $12.

Westbury

Settled in the 1820s, Westbury still has the atmosphere of the Nineteenth Century with a famous village green that is used for fetes and other celebrations. The White House is a fine local National Trust building. Built about 1841, it is furnished in early English oak and includes a fine collection of Staffordshire china and a local history display. Open Tues, Thurs, Sat and Sun 10am-4pm, and by appointment. Adults $4, children $3, family $14.
4 ensuites, double B&B $60-75.

North-Western Tasmania

The north-west corner of Tasmania is a land of spectacular capes and coastal scenery, rich paddocks over rolling hills, almost untouched wilderness areas and historic mining towns. The first Europeans to see the North-West Coast were Lieutenant Matthew Flinders and Surgeon George Bass on their epic circumnavigation of Van Diemen's Land in 1798-1799. Settlement began in the 1820s with the formation of the Van Diemen's Land Company. As the countryside was cleared, it became an exporter of timber, agricultural goods and beef. The continued prosperity of the North-west was assisted by the discovery of the richest tin mine in the world by "Philosopher" Smith in 1871. Other mining discoveries helped the area to develop rapidly. In 1937 Associated Pulp and Paper Mills (APPM) was established at Burnie, heralding an era of rapid industrial expansion.

Apart from the coast, much of the North-west is inaccessible to the average visitor. Only a few roads strike their way through the wilderness to isolated mining towns. There are no completely sealed roads linking the far north-west at Marrawah or Smithton with the central West coast towns of Zeehan, Queenstown and Strahan. You have to take a ferry, *The Fatman,* over the Pieman River to traverse the road between Corinna and Zeehan.

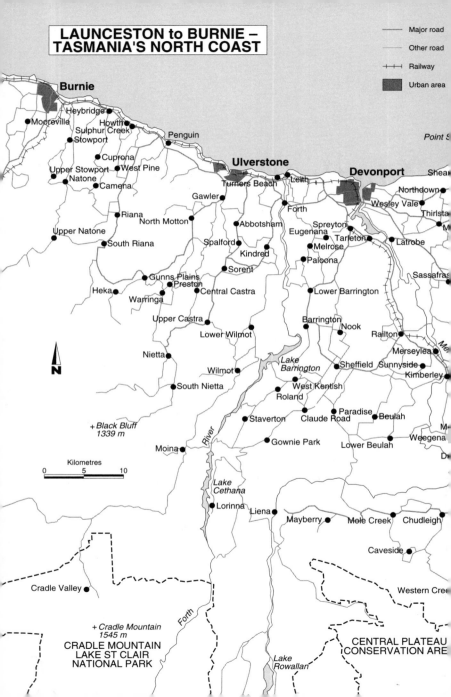

DEVONPORT

Devonport is a town of about 25,000 people situated on the north coast of Tasmania, where the Mersey River enters Bass Strait. The fourth largest city in Tasmania, it is the gateway for the car and passenger ferries from the Mainland. It was originally two towns that voted to amalgamate in 1893: Formby on the west bank of the river, and Torquay on the east bank. Devonport had its beginnings as the centre of a rich agricultural and orchard area. Today, the Mersey Valley remains one of Tasmania's main orchard districts, but is now also famous for its mushrooms.

Tourist information

The Devonport Visitors Centre, 92 Formby Road, (03) 6424-4466, is located across the Mersey River from the Spirit of Tasmania Terminal.

ACCOMMODATION

Here is a selection of accommodation with prices for a double room per night. This should be used as a guide only. Most of the hotels face Bass Strait and have a very pleasant aspect.

Gateway Motor Inn, 16 Fenton Street, **(03) 6424-4922**
64 ensuites, licensed restaurant, double $98-113.

Sunrise Motor Inn, 140 North Fenton Street, **(03) 6424-1631,**
33 ensuites, double $96-131.

Argosy Motor Inn, 221 Tarleton Street, East Devonport,
(03) 6427-8872,
37 ensuites, licensed restaurant, double $72.

Birchmore, 10 Oldaker Street, 6 rooms with ensuite (B&B) with roomy apartments and fax etc facilities, double $100.

Edgewater Motor Inn, 2 Thomas Street, East Devonport, **(03) 6427-8441;**
29 ensuites, licensed restaurant, double $50.

Elimatta, 15 Victoria Parade, **(03) 6424-6555,**
22 ensuites, licensed restaurant, double $55.

Glasgow Lodge, 59 George Street, **(03) 6424 1480,**
self contained holiday units fit four comfortably, near the beach, double $90.

Formby Hotel, 82 Formby Road, **(03) 6424-1601,**
12 ensuites, licensed restaurant, double B&B $50-65.

Devonport Vacation Village, Caroline Street, East Devonport, **(03) 6427-8886,**
22 unites, double $40-55.

Mersey Bluff Caravan Park, Mersey Bluff, **(03) 6424-8655,**
caravan double $40, cabin double $50, camping - powered site $15 double, unpowered sites $13.00 double.

Abel Tasman Caravan Park, 6 Wright Street, East Devonport, **(03) 6427-8794,**
caravan double $30-35 ($6 per adult extra), cabin double $48-56, camping - powered site $14 double, unpowered sites $10.00 double.

EATING OUT

Devonport has a good selection of restaurants, and several hotels have counter meals. Coffee shops and takeaway outlets abound. Here are a few you might like to try.

Autograph, Mersey Bluff, **(03) 6424-2204.**
Water views over the Bass Strait, licensed.

Mallee Grill, 161 Rooke Street, **(03) 6424-4477.**
Great steaks. Licensed.

New Mandarin Inn, 156 William Street, **(03) 6424-4398.**
 Chinese fare, BYO.

El Mecciko, 24 King Street, **(03) 6423-5455.**
Spicy Mexican dining, licensed and BYO.

Rialto Gallery, 159 Rooke Street, **(03) 6424-6793.**
Italian dining in a gallery setting, licensed and BYO.

SIGHTSEEING

The ferry *Torquay* makes the crossing between East Devonport near the ferry terminal and West Devonport, near The Brickworks every half hour.

The Victoria Bridge connects East Devonport to Devonport, and it is 2 km downstream from the ferry terminal. To get to the bridge follow Formby Road along the river bank. Walking and bicycle tracks circle the city and are found along the eastern shore. Bicycles can be hired at Mersey Bluff during the season, and the Visitors Centre can advise of places at other times.

Mersey Bluff is one of only thirteen major sites where rock carvings by the Tasmanian Aboriginals can be viewed. Tiagarra Tasmanian Aboriginal Culture and Art Centre at the Bluff headland has dramatic dioramas of the way of life of these people. It is open daily, except for July when it is closed for renovations. Adults $3, children $2. The Devonport Maritime Museum, 47 Victoria Parade, was formerly the Harbour Master's residence and Pilot Station, built in about 1920. It now has exhibits of Devonport and North-west Coastal Maritime History, with fine detailed models from the days of sail and steam to the modern passenger ferries. Open Tues-Sun, 2-4pm. Adults $3, children $1, family $5.

Mersey River at sunset, Devonport.

Devonport Gallery and Arts Centre is in the middle of the city at 45-47 Stewart Street. The lovely old converted church has the latest exhibitions, and is open Mon-Fri 10am-5pm, Sun 2-5pm (closed Sat).

Victoria Parade is a scenic garden walk that follows the river and sea to Mersey Bluff. There is a good swimming beach, children's playground, kiosk and public toilets.

Taswegia Historic Printery and Craft Gallery, 57 Formby Road, (03) 6424-8300, is an Historic Printery and Craft Gallery, and is open daily 10am-5pm. It has one of Australasia's largest heritage collection of print technology dating from 1852, and all in working condition. Taswegia specialises in the production of early colonial charts, convict documents, paintings, maps and paraphernalia. It also has an exclusive range of giftware including printed linen, fabrics, woodcrafts, ceramics, pottery, posters, books and many other interesting and decorative items. Adults $2, children 50.

Home Hill, 77 Middle Road. This was the family home of Prime Minister Joseph Lyons and Dame Enid Lyons, Australia's first woman member of the House of Representatives, and the author of several books. They built the house in 1916 and lived there for the rest of their lives, apart from a period of five years. Dame Enid passed away in 1981, and the home is now operated by the City Council in conjunction with the National Trust. Home Hill is as Dame Enid left it and contains many interesting and historic mementoes. It is open on Tues, Wed, Thurs, Sat and Sun 2-4pm. Adult $6, children $3; family $12.

The Don River Railway, off Bass Highway on the road to Ulverstone. This is an operating railway museum, and is open daily throughout the year, with steam trains running hourly every Sunday and public holiday afternoons. The museum has the largest collection of steam locomotives in Tasmania, dating from 1879 to 1951, and the largest collection of passenger carriages dating from 1869 to 1961. Adults $7, children $4.

OUTLYING AREAS

Deloraine

Set amidst rolling hills midway between Launceston and Devonport is this charming colonial town, which has also been classified by the National Trust. Many of the buildings date back to the 1830s.

Among the many attractions in the district are the King Solomon and Marakoopa Caves near Mole Creek. Marakoopa Cave is part of the Wilderness World Heritage Area. It is a wet cave with two small rivers flowing through it and illuminated glow-worms. King Solomon is smaller, but dry, with impressive pillars, cathedral chambers and light-reflecting crystals. These world renowned limestone caves are open every day. Inspection times. For King Solomon Cave — 10.30am, 11.30am, 12.30pm, 2pm, 3pm and 4pm. For Marakoopa Cave — 10am, 11.15am, 1pm, 2.30pm and 4pm. Admission: adults $8; children $4; family $20.

There are good walking tracks at the Great Western Tiers, dolerite cliffs which rise sharply from the coastal plains. There is quite a variety of vegetation, with myrtle in sheltered river valleys, King Billy pine on the upper slopes and alpine woodland on the Central

Plateau. The Liffey Forest Reserve has several places for picnics and short walks. The Meander Forest Reserve, about 30 minutes' drive from Deloraine, has a number of waterfalls and spectacular views, but the walks are longer and more difficult.

Latrobe

Situated 10 km east of the Bass Strait ferry terminal, and 5 km south of the airport, Latrobe was one of the first towns established on the North-west Coast. The Mersey River with its willow-lined banks flows through the town. In recent years the town has been classified as an historic town, and has developed a small but sophisticated restaurant and specialty boutique trade. They say that it has the most restaurants and cafes per head of population in Australia.

Port Sorell

The port is 19 km east of Devonport on the picturesque Rubicon River estuary. It is a popular holiday resort with prolific native flora and fauna, and good swimming and boating are available at nearby Hawley Beach. Nearby attractions include the Bass Strait beaches and the Asbestos Range National Park.

Sheffield

Standing guard over Sheffield and dominating the skyline is 1231 metre-high Mt Roland which seems to rise straight out of the rolling countryside. It is a spectacular backdrop for this town of around 5000 people with a surprisingly vigorous artistic life. A feature which draws many tourists is the spectacular murals that feature the district's pioneer history and make Sheffield an outdoor art gallery. Sheffield is also the gateway to the Lake Barrington International Rowing Course, where world championships were held in 1990. The lake is part of the Mersey Forth hydro-electric development, with seven power stations and seven man-made lakes.

Lake Barrington is accessible by bitumen road which goes through some rugged mountain country. If you have your own equipment, the lake is ideal for a range of water sports including rowing, water skiing, power boating, canoeing and model yachting. There are launching ramps on both sides of the lake, but it is necessary to book the rowing course with the ranger. The recreation area of the park is open daily from 8am until dusk, and facilities include a large day visitor shelter with wood barbecues, seats and tables, and a kiosk which is only open on weekends throughout the summer.

Ulverstone

About 20 km west of Devonport is the prosperous seaside town of Ulverstone. It is the business centre of rich agricultural country reaching south from the sea to the mountains. Safe and extensive beaches and river, woodlands, and mountain resorts provide ideal conditions for people to stay a while. The town is the woodchopping centre of Australia. It is said that the sport began in 1870 when two bushmen got into an argument in a local pub about who was the best man with an axe. With a wager of 50 at stake, they adjourned to a nearby paddock to settle the matter and the sport was born. In 1974, the world championship was held in Ulverstone. Dominating the town is the Shrine of Remembrance, the unique World War II memorial clock tower. Three columns linked by bronze chains rising from a map of Tasmania represent the Australian Army, Navy and Air Force. The whole edifice is topped by a torch representing the Flame of Remembrance. Caves and Gunns Plains are some of the chief attractions of the Ulverstone district. A round trip to Gunns Plains, which is the site of a new hop industry, also traverses magnificent rural, mountain and river scenery. The spectacular Leven Canyon, about 40 km from Ulverstone through Netta must be visited. A short walk takes the visitor to a lookout over a breathtaking 250 metre sheer drop down to the Leven River.

Penguin

The town of Penguin, 12 km further west, was named after the fairy penguin colonies along the coastline. It is situated on three bays which provide safe beaches for bathing and picnicking. It is best to take the Scenic Drive (old Bass Highway) between Penguin and Ulverstone for the superb views of rugged coastal scenery, including the off-shore islets which are bird sanctuaries. A feature of the Penguin Municipality is the ambitious Dial Range Regional Sports Complex, catering for most sports, plus bushwalking.

BURNIE

Burnie is a thriving city of 20,000 people, and an important industrial centre and deep water port which handles more than 2 million tons of cargo each year. It is the terminal for ANL sea road vessels, and trades directly with more than 40 overseas ports. Burnie is also at the centre of a lush dairying area and is surrounded by a wide forest belt that runs parallel with the coastline, about 50 km inland. About 22 million super feet of quality timber is produced each year from this area.

The distance from Launceston along the Bass Highway is 150 km which takes about 2.5 hours. From Queenstown the distance is 176 km which again takes around 2.5 hours. The drive from Smithton 86 km away takes 1.5 hours. Burnie is well serviced by coach as well.

Tourist information

The Tasmanian Visitor Information Centre is at Civic Square precinct, off Little Alexander Street, **(03) 6434-6111.** It is in the same building as the Pioneer Village Museum.

ACCOMMODATION

Burnie has a number of good hotels, motels, holiday flats and caravan parks. Prices do vary depending on the standard of accommodation and the season. In the selection below we give prices for a double room per night which should be used as a guide only.

Top of the Town Hotel Motel, 195 Mount Street, Upper Burnie, **(03) 6431-4444;**
30 ensuites, licensed restaurant, sauna. Double $75.

Wellers Inn, 36 Queen Street, **(03) 6431-1088;**
25 units, children's play area, licensed restaurant; double $95-128.

Burnie Town House, 139 Wilson Street, **(03) 6431-4455;**
52 ensuites; licensed restaurant; double $95.

The Beach Hotel, 1 Wilson Street, **(03) 6431 2333,**
16 ensuite, friendly and clean, counter meals, double $60.

Treasure Island Caravan Park, 253 Bass Highway, Cooee, **(03) 6431-1925;**
hostel double $24-28; caravan double $36; cabin double $54, camping powered sites $14 double, unpowered $10 double.

EATING OUT

Burnie has some spectacular views and the restaurants make the most of them.

Weller's Inn, 36 Queen Street, **(03) 6431-1088.**
On top of a hill with spreading views. Renowned for its sea food.

The Burnleigh, 8 Alexander Street, **(03) 6431-3947.**
Historic home surroundings with excellent food. BYO.

Raindrop Rest (in the Beachfront Voyager), North Terrace, **(03)6431-4866.**
Views over the Bass Strait.

Mallee Grill (in the Regent Hotel), North Terrace, **(03) 6431-1933.**
Upmarket counter meals on the waterfront.

Rialto Gallery Restaurant, 254 Mount Street, **(03) 6431-7718.**
Excellent Italian food in an art gallery.

SIGHTSEEING

The Pioneer Village Museum in High Street, Civic Centre Plaza, is Burnie's premier attraction. It is close to the centre of the city, and the entire village is under one roof. It has more than 30,000 individual items on display. There is an inn, newspaper office, general store, blacksmith shop, and many authentic replicas of a commercial centre of the 1890-1910 period. Open Mon-Fri, 10am-5pm, and Sat-Sun 1.30-5pm. Adults $4.50; children $1.50. The tea rooms are a popular spot to have a cappuccino or a glass of wine.

Burnie Park is only a few minutes' walk away. It has shady trees, a rose garden and the old Burnie Inn which was first licensed in 1847. It is the oldest building in the city, and is open daily for inspection during the summer. They only sell light refreshments and Devonshire Teas — a little different from days of yore. There is also an animal sanctuary. The Burnie Regional Art Gallery in Wilmot Street, open Mon-Fri, 9am-5pm, Sat-Sun, 1.30-4.30pm, displays one of the finest collections of Australian contemporary art in Tasmania. Admission free.

The AMCOR Paper Mill, Marine Terrace, (03) 6430-7777, has free guided tours at 2pm Mon-Fri. Children under the age of 12 are not admitted, and women are asked to wear slacks and low heeled shoes. Booking is essential. Amcor is Australia's largest manufacturer of fine papers. The tour includes the pulp mill, bleaching plant, paper machine rooms and the paper finishing and warehouse areas.

The Fernglade Forest Reserve is a lovely side trip to a park where you can see platypuses. A great place to have lunch. The Lactos Cheese Factory, Old Surry Road, (03) 642566, is the biggest cheese company in Tasmania. It has tastings Mon-Fri, 9am-4.30pm. Admission free.

WYNYARD

About 16 km from Burnie with a population of around 4500 people, Wynyard is a pretty town, and is almost more English than England. The town is located on the Inglis River, and the airport for Burnie is found here. It is a major gateway to the North-west coast and offers panoramic views, while Fossil Buff (just beyond the Wynyard Golf Course) is a unique area rich in rare and ancient fossils, including Australia's oldest marsupials. The waters around the town are popular with divers and underwater photographers because of their clarity. Equipment for scuba diving can be hired in town.

ACCOMMODATION

Alexandria Guest House, Table Cape Road, **(03) 6442-2094,** double B&B $85-96.

Wynyard Caravan Park, The Esplanade, **(03) 6442-1998,** cabin double $50-55, caravan double $$32-35, hostel double $22-24, camping powered sites $14 double, unpowered $10 double.

INLAND SIGHTS

Hellyer Gorge

The gorge is about 50 km from Burnie on the Waratah Highway, which links the North-west with the west coast. It is a mountainous scenic reserve with thick myrtle forest.

Waratah

About 80 km from Burnie (via Hellyer gorge) is the historic mining town of Waratah. It was here in 1871 that James "Philosopher" Smith discovered the Mount Bischoff tin ore body. The scarred slopes are a reminder that it was once the richest tin mine in the world. The mine was opened in 1888 with an investment capital of $58,000 and paid dividends of $2 million. The mine closed in 1946 and today it is a rugged outcrop of colourful rocks honey-combed with tunnels and shafts. A few miners still fossick for minerals in the area. An audio display for visitors is located at Smith's Hut opposite the Council Chambers and the Waratah and Gift Shop. The rain water from Waratah is reputed to be the purest in the world.

Savage River

Low-grade iron-ore was found in this region in 1877, but it was nearly 100 years before extraction became economical. Savage River is a company town, 125 km from Wynyard, which was built to accommodate about 1500 people working in the Savage River open cut iron mine. The ore is crushed, concentrated and pumped in a slurry over an 85 km pipeline to the Port Latta plant near Stanley on the North-west coast. It is possible to book tours of the mine, (03) 6471-6225. Visitors can watch the 85-tonne haul trucks and the crushing operation.

Corinna

Once a tough gold rush town with 2500 people, Corinna sprawls over both sides of the Pieman River. The town gets its name from the Aboriginal word for the thylacine (Tasmanian tiger), and lies about 150 km from Burnie (via Hellyer Gorge). It is now almost a ghost town with a few facilities for tourists. The largest nugget of gold ever found in Tasmania, weighing 243 ounces, was found in the nearby Rocky River. The Pieman River is said to owe its name to Alexander Pearce, a pie man from Hobart who was gaoled for selling tainted pies. In 1822 and 1823 he escaped and was recaptured after killing and eating his companions.

The Pieman River Cruise from Corinna to the Pieman Heads on the M.V. Arcadia II is quite worthwhile (03) 6446-1170. Adults $33; children 5-15 $16, including morning tea. The four-hour cruise leaves every day at 10.30am.

The Parks and Wildlife Service has set up a couple of easy walks to investigate the unique rainforest vegetation. The Slender Tree

Fern walk takes only about 15 minutes; the Whyte River walk takes about 90 minutes and passes by a 1200-year-old Huon pine and a beautiful stand of blackwood.

ALONG THE COAST

Boat Harbour

This attractive town about 16 km from Wynyard is a popular resort. The view from the road that leads down the hill from the farming hinterland is one of blue-green seas and fine white sands. The crystal-clear water is ideal for underwater photography.

Rocky Cape National Park

About 30 km east from Wynyard is Rocky Cape National Park, the smallest of Tasmania's National Parks. Some of its geological formations are 700 million years old. It also contains some of the richest Aboriginal sites in Tasmania. Within caves in the cliff faces, midden deposits of shells, bone, stone and charcoal have been undisturbed by natural forces. Archaeologists believe that human occupation of the caves began about 8000 years ago. Food there was always plentiful and the area appears to have been a convenient stopping place for Aboriginal groups. The establishment of the Van Diemen's Land Company in the 1820s, however, brought the Aboriginal history of Rocky Cape to an abrupt end, since the settlements disrupted their seasonal movements. Two of the most impressive Aboriginal shelters are just a short walk from the car park. There are also some interesting caves, and several bushwalks in the park. The walk from Sisters Beach to Rocky Cape is noted for its spring displays of wildflowers. No camping is allowed in the park.

Stanley

The dominant feature of Stanley is The Nut, Tasmania's answer to Ayers Rock, a 150 metre rocky outcrop with a 35 hectare summit that dominates the coastal scenery for many kilometres around.

The Nut is connected to the mainland by an isthmus about 7 km long, and if you wish to climb it, there is an easy walking track which begins opposite the post office and ends at the summit cairn. Or you can take the chairlift that operates from the rear of the Nut Shop Tea Rooms. Adults $6, children $4, family $15.

Stanley was the site of the first settlement in North-west Tasmania and it has changed very little since then. It has a wealth of nineteenth and early Twentieth Century buildings, many of which have become visitor attractions and accommodation. The Plough Inn, for instance, is a lovely Georgian structure which has become an arts and crafts shop. In the graveyard are buried surveyor Henry Hellyer and the talented architect and magistrate John Lee Archer, whose distinguished buildings have left their mark on Hobart and the Midlands.

You can also inspect Lyons Cottage, the birthplace of Tasmanian Premier and Australian Prime Minister Joseph Lyons (open 10am-4pm daily, admission free). The home of the chief agent of the Van Diemen's Land Company, Highfield, has also been classified as an historic site. If you have time, you may wish to visit the Stanley Discovery Centre in Church Street. Open daily 10am-4.30pm. Adults $3, children 50.

Smithton

The administration of the Circular Head Municipality of the far North-west is based at Smithton. It has a large modern butter factory as well as a bacon factory, a large piggery and several saw mills. The district has an ideal climate for growing peas, and the town boasts of a pea freezing factory. Air services connect Smithton with King Island, and aerial tours of the many shore islands may be booked at the airport. Lacrum Dairy Farm, (03) 6452-2322, is 6 km west of Smithton. Visitors are welcome to this 275ha property, where they have a Wombat Tarn, picnic and barbecue facilities, bush walks, and milking between 3pm-5.30pm every day from October to the end of June. Adults $7.50, children $5.

Driving directly south, you can visit Allendale Gardens at Edith Creek (botanical gardens in miniature), Balfour Track Reserve, Julius River Reserve, Lake Chisholm, West Beckett Reserve and Milkshake Hill Forest Reserve. You would have to do this independently, though, as there are no guided tours to these parts.

Woolnorth
In the North-westernmost corner of Tasmania is Woolnorth, a sprawling pastoral property with 34 km of ocean frontage. It is the remaining holding of the Van Diemen's Land Company which was founded in 1825 by Royal Charter of King George IV. The countryside is pretty, but rugged — the last four Tasmanian Tigers in captivity were caught in 1908 in the backblocks of Woolnorth.
   Woolnorth provides day tours for groups of tourists. They have a multitude of displays, activities and walks, and refreshments are available.

Marrawah
Situated at the western end of the Bass Highway, 48 km from Smithton, is the settlement of Marrawah, the westernmost town in Tasmania. It is well worth a visit as wildflowers and native fauna are plentiful. There are several important Aboriginal rock carvings at Mount Cameron a little to the north. The carvings of circles and bird tracks are similar to ones found in the deserts of the Australian mainland.

The West Coast

The rugged wilderness of the West Coast draws tourists from all over the world. The rainforest, the wild hills, the tea-coloured rivers, the immense trees, the wind-swept beaches make you feel as though you have left civilisation behind for ever. The few people who live here are clustered in a few small settlements based on mining or fishing.

Tullah

The tiny town of Tullah is about 110 km from Burnie and 50 km from Queenstown. The Hydro-Electric Commission once used it as a base for its power developments; now it is an ideal spot to use as a base for exploring the wilderness areas of the West Coast. The Wee Georgie Wood is the only operational steam locomotive on the West Coast and offers a real thrill for the kids as they travel along the 1.6 km track. Adults $2, children $1, family $5.

Rosebery *(Map at front)*

Rosebery is a town of about 1,600 which consistently tops the State as the town with the highest average income. It is supported by the Pasminco mine which once produced gold, lead and zinc, but now only zinc, which is shipped to Hobart for processing. There are three two-hour tours each day at 9.30am, 12.30pm and 3.30pm. Visitors can view the zinc mine surface area. For information ring **(03) 6473-1247.** Adults $8, children $5,

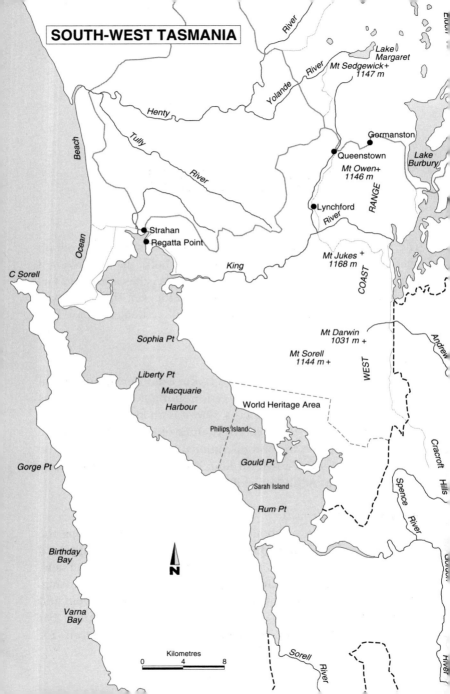

pensioner/student $7, family $24. About 10 minutes outside the town are 104 metre-high Montezuma Falls, the highest in the State - well worth the short hike to see them.

ZEEHAN *(Map at front)*

Thirty-three kilometres north of Queenstown is the town of Zeehan. Its name comes from a nearby mountain which was named after the flagship of Abel Tasman by Bass and Flinders in 1798. Over the years its fortunes have fluctuated wildly as prices rose and fell and technologies developed. The boom came when rich silver-lead deposits were discovered in 1882 by a prospector named Frank Long. Frank never benefited from his find, but by the turn of the century Zeehan became the third largest settlement in Tasmania, a town of 10,000 which could afford to bring in Dame Nellie Melba and Enrico Caruso. But the ore ran out and before World War I the town began to decline. A number of buildings have survived from the glory days, including the Gaiety Theatre, St Luke's Church and the Post Office.

The excellent West Coast Pioneers' Memorial Museum is housed in the old School of Mines, and is divided into five main categories of exhibits — a mineral collection; historical items relating to the West Coast; modern mining on the West Coast; locomotives and tracked mining equipment; and exhibits of Tasmanian animals and birds, with artefacts of Tasmanian Aborigines. Adults $5, children $3, family $10. Places to visit around Zeehan include Trial Harbour (20 km), Heemskirk Falls (19 km), Granville Harbour (40 km) and the Lower Pieman Dam (50 km). Both harbours are popular with fishermen seeking crayfish and abalone.

ACCOMMODATION

Prices are per night and indicative only.

Heemskirk Motor Hotel, **(03) 6471 6107,**
33 ensuites modern style, restaurant, double $80.
Hemskirk Motor Inn, older building nearby, 18 ensuite but no
phone etc, double $60.

Hotel Cecil, Main Street, **(03) 6471 6221,**
8 rooms shared facilities, restaurant, double $65.
Old Miners Cottages, same phone number, 4 two bedroom
cottages, double $80.

QUEENSTOWN

Queenstown, with a population of about 4000, is located on the
rugged west coast of Tasmania. It rains here 320 days out of 365
and the annual rainfall is over three metres. The locals are tough:
the football ground has a gravel surface, the only one in Australia,
as the cold wet winters make turf unsuitable. It wasn't sunshine,
but minerals, which brought civilisation to Queenstown.

Queenstown is firstly and lastly a mining town. After seeing so
many trees along the way, your first glimpse may come as a shock
because the hills around the town are denuded of greenery. This
has been caused by a combination of tree felling, sulphur fumes,
fire and heavy rain. As the Lyell Highway descends steeply into
Queenstown via the Linda Valley, there is a panoramic view of
naked hills strewn with multi-coloured boulders which reflect the
sun's rays. In the evening, the setting sun causes the mountains
and hills to change from shades of brilliant gold to hues of deep
pink. It is an unforgettable sight. With the decline of mining,
Queenstown has taken up tourism. Its desolate landscape is now
described as having "outstanding heritage value" and being "a
visual and psychological icon" or "one of the great cultural
landscapes of Tassie".

The history of Queenstown is fascinating. In 1883, two prospectors who had only arrived in the Linda Valley the day before discovered a strange iron outcrop which rose about 25 feet above the surface. This was the famous Iron Blow, where mining of the riches of Mt Lyell began. About two weeks later, the diggers pegged out a fifty-acre lease, in the centre of which was the Blow. They suspected that the Blow was the source of the gold they washed in the creek below the outcrop. The Blow was worked as a gold mine for ten years, with everybody ignoring the millions of pounds of copper in it. The Mount Lyell gold mine was bought by Bowes Kelly in 1891, and he formed the Mt Lyell Mining Company in Melbourne. But in that year gold mining at Mt Lyell came to an end, although it has always remained a welcome by-product. The directors of the company brought Edward Dyer Peters, a world authority on copper smelting, from the USA, and he conducted a successful smelting trial at the Argenton smelter, 6.5 km south of Zeehan.

The Mt Lyell Mining and Railway Company, one of the oldest mining companies in Australia, was formed in 1893, after the previous company had been dissolved for financial reasons. The new company failed to raise enough money for an extensive development program, and mining at the Blow nearly came to a stop. Then an incredibly rich silver seam with an average of over a thousand ounces of silver to the ton was discovered by Dr Peters. This lucky discovery helped the young company out of its financial difficulties.

In 1895, Robert Carl Sticht, another American, but this time a metallurgist, was given a free hand by the directors of the company to design the first Mt Lyell smelters. His pyritic smelting process, which represented an important advance in the technology of copper smelting, became famous and was copied in many countries. By 1891, the little shanty town of Penghana had sprung up around the smelters, but in 1896 it was wiped out by fire. The refugees set up home in a newly planned town on the banks of the Queen River, and called it, appropriately enough,

Queenstown. Mount Lyell had a long history and is now in its dying days, with a succession of owners opening, closing and re-opening it. Nowadays, however, there is some possibility of living off tourism as Queenstown attracts thousands of tourists each year for its unique combination of untamed wilderness, lunar landscape and mining history.

Redline Coaches have services between Hobart, Burnie, Strahan and Queenstown. By road, Queenstown is 254 km north-west of Hobart along the Lyell Highway, and 175 km south-west of Burnie along the Waratah and Zeehan Highways. Visitor information can be obtained from the hotels and motels in the area. There is a City Guide map in Driffield Street at the end of Orr Street.

EATING OUT

If you are a serious gastronome, you might want to press on for another 45 minutes to Strahan. However, apart from takeaways, there are some decent restaurants in Queenstown:

Silver Hills, Penghana Road, **(03) 6471-1755.**
A chance to relax with restaurant fare.

Empire Hotel, 2 Orr Street, **(03) 6471-1699.**
Hearty counter meals.

ACCOMMODATION

Westcoaster Motor Inn, Batchelor Street, **(03) 6471-1033,**
60 ensuites, licensed restaurant, double $62-85.

Silver Hills Motel, Penghana Road, **(03) 6471-1755,** 56 ensuites,
licensed restaurant, double $50-78.

Mt Lyell Motor Inn, cnr Orr and Driffield Streets, **(03) 6471-1888,**
40 ensuites, licensed restaurant, double $60.

Queenstown Cabin and Tourist Park, 17 Grafton Street,
(03) 6471-1332,
cabin double $60, caravan double $35, camping powed sites $15
double, unpowered sites $8 double.

SIGHTSEEING

An historic tour walk has been mapped out around the town, and
information plaques have been erected at places of interest. No
stay in Queenstown would be complete without a visit to the Mt
Lyell Mine. Guided tours are available and depart from the
Western Arts & Crafts Centre. Tours are of approximately two
hours' duration, and include viewing the mine workings and the
recently established Mining Museum. Tour times: October to
April—9.15am, 2.30pm, 4.30pm; May to September—9.15am,
4pm. Additional tours during peak season. Adults $10, children
U16 $5.50, (03) 6471-2388.

The Eric Thomas Galley Museum, cnr Driffield and Sticht Streets,
features displays of old photographs dealing with the West Coast,
as well as items of household equipment and personal effects in
use during the early days. The museum is open daily. Adults $4;
children $2.50.

In the Museum is the HEC Information Centre, which has
information on the King and Anthony Power Development, and
the HEC Guided Tours Field Liaison Office, which can arrange
guided tours of the areas opened up by construction of access
roads for the West Coast Power Developments.

Miners Siding in Driffield Street is a Queenstown Centenary Park
Development, and incorporates the Miners Sunday Sculpture by
Stephen Walker. The sculpture is made of bronze and Huon Pine,
and depicts an early miner and his family on the day of rest, and
the changes that transformed a rough miners' camp to a town and
community.

Part of the Miners Siding Park has been developed as a rainforest, with many species that occur mainly in Western Tasmania. Also in the Park is a restored ABT Locomotive, which was part of the system that was the only transport link between Queenstown and the outside world until 1932. Iron Blow, the original gold mine, is situated north of the town at Gormanston, 2 km off the Lyell Highway. The site has been developed as an area of historic and scenic interest, and offers excellent panoramic views over the mountains and Linda Valley.

The Crotty and South West Access Road turns off the Lyell Highway 10 km north of the town, and was once the railway line for the North Lyell Copper Company. It provides access to the Darwin Meteorite Crater, the Franklin River, Fincham Park, Kelly Basin, the King Power Development and Crotty Camp. Information on the area is available from the HEC Information Centre in Queenstown.

Lake Margaret, north of Queenstown, was one of Tasmania's first hydro electric schemes and was built and owned by the Mt Lyell Company in 1914. The station and village remain as they were in the 1900s, with the original machines still working. A 2134 metres wooden stave pipeline still delivers water from the lake to the Penstock, and a walk up the hill provides great views of the rugged West Coast - if it isn't raining, for this is the rainiest spot in the whole State.

On the Zeehan Highway, 14 km from Queenstown, there is a balancing rock which gives an insight into the unique geology of the area. The parking area here offers views over the glacial valleys of the Henty and Yolande Rivers. There are information plaques, and a sign-post to the rock.

STRAHAN

Once a sleepy fishing and mining town, Strahan is a prosperous and sophisticated village of about 550 people which has become one of Tasmania's main tourist attractions, as the gateway to the State's fabulous rainforest and as an important site in Australia's history. It was named Tasmania's premier tourist town in 1995. History and forest are linked, in a way, for Strahan's renaissance began in 1982 when it was the pivot point for the "Fight for the Franklin" controversy over the State Government's plan to dam the Gordon below Franklin. There are only two safe anchorages on the West Coast, Strahan on Macquarie Harbour and Port Davey further south. Macquarie Harbour is larger than Sydney Harbour, but Hell's Gate, the entrance, is only 200 metres wide. The sea becomes a frothing torrent as it rushes through the heads. Since there were large forests of Huon Pine in the Strahan area, it soon attracted the attention of the early colonists. In 1821 a prison was established on Sarah Island in Macquarie Harbour. It was there that the colonial "gulag" was its most brutal. The prisoners sent there were the worst of the worst and the administration was terribly brutal. The records show that of 182 prisoners in 1822, 169 received 7000 lashes, an average of 40 each. It was from here, and not Port Arthur, that Marcus Clarke drew the material for the gothic horrors of his novel *For the Term of His Natural Life*. The prison was finally closed in 1833 and the buildings were allowed to decay. Sarah Island is now a National Trust historic site. The innovative Strahan Visitors Centre is a museum displaying the history of the region. Its claim is that inside "the lifeblood of the wild west throbs painfully, joyfully, evocatively in a living, breathing display of a community's dreams". A hard act to follow — but it is worthwhile. Admission: adults $4.50; children free; family $9.

The Customs House was opened in 1900 and built in grand style. It still exhibits much of its original Huon pine and blackwood fittings. The stately home of Ormiston, built in 1902, is one of the finest examples of Federation architecture in Australia. Strahan Cemetery provides an insight into the lives of Strahan's early settlers. Many of the early tombstones were made out of the nearly indestructible Huon pine and have weathered the intemperate West Coast rain and winds. Ocean Beach is the longest beach in Tasmania, stretching for over 30 km from Macquarie Heads in the south to Trial Harbour in the north. It is an ideal spot to watch thousands of muttonbirds returning to their rookeries at dusk. The Henty Dunes are a series of 30 metre high dunes about 14 km out of town which are well worth exploring. And, of course, Sarah Island can be visited by commercial tour boat or by private boat.

From Strahan you can take a flights over the peak, rapids, gorges and bush by plane or helicopter. If you can afford it, this is a must.

Seair Adventure Charters, (03) 6471-7718, offer scenic plane and helicopter flights over Frenchman's Cap, the Franklin and Gordon Rivers and Cradle Mountain and Lake St Clair. A 45-minute flight costs about $90 per person; a 65-minute flight about $130.

Wilderness Air Seaplanes, (03) 6471-7280, offer flights over the Gordon River, Frenchman's Cap, Hells Gate and Ocean Beach for about $99 per person. They also land on the Gordon River itself.

Cruises

There are several cruises of Macquarie Harbour, the Gordon River and the area around Strahan. These are a real must because you get a taste of the grandeur of the wilderness. For detailed information, consult a Tasmanian Visitor Information Centre.

Gordon River Cruises, **(03) 6471-7187,**

depart daily from Strahan Wharf. Half-day cruises: adults $45; children $25. Full-day cruises (9am to 3.30pm): adults $61; children $31.

World Heritage Cruises, **(03) 6471-7174,**

depart daily from Strahan Wharf. Full-day cruises with lunch: adults $44; children $20.

ACCOMMODATION

Accommodation for all budgets is plentiful in Strahan now that it has become a major tourist attraction, but most of the establishments are small self-contained units. Book ahead.

Franklin Manor, The Esplanade, **(03) 6471-7311,**
18 ensuites, double B&B $135-195.

Strahan Youth Hostel, Harvey Street, **(03) 6471-7255,**
58 guests, double $24-29.

Strahan Village, The Esplanade, **(03) 6471-7191,**
is the largest establishment in town. Hotel-style, 36 ensuites, double $115-165. Motel-style, 61 ensuites, double $85-115.

Sharonlee Strahan Villas, Andrew Street, West Strahan,
(03) 6471-7224,
15 ensuites, double $85-110.

Strahan Wilderness Lodge, Ocean Beach Road, **(03) 6471-7142,**
5 ensuites, double B&B $45-55.

Strahan Central, 1 Harold Street, **(03) 6471-7612,**
3 ensuites, double $110-140.

Gordon Gateway Chalet, Grining Street, Regatta Point,
(03) 6471-7165,
12 ensuites, double $65-140.

EATING OUT

Ormiston House, The Esplanade, **(03) 6471-7077.**
Five-star dining in lovely Federation rooms. Duck and crayfish are specialties. Licensed; special 3-course for about $41.

Franklin Manor, The Esplanade, **(03) 6471-7311.**
Five-star dining in a casual atmosphere. Licensed; special 3-course for about $41.

Hamers Bar and Grill, The Esplanade **(03) 6471-7191.**
Bistro-style family meals with extensive range. Try their venison pie. Licensed.

Strahan Central, 1 Harold Street, **(03) 6471-7612.**
Reasonable prices for home-style cooking.

Regatta Point Tavern, Regatta Point, **(03) 6471-7103.**
Pub-style family meals.

World Heritage areas

"The natural world contains an unbelievable diversity, and offers a variety of choices, provided, of course, that we retain some of this world and that we live in the matter that permits us to go out, seek it, find it, and make these choices. We must try to retain as much as possible of what still remains of the unique, rare and beautiful. Tasmania can be a shining beacon..."

These words of Olegas Truchanas, the migrant who made Tasmania his home and became one of the most eloquent spokesmen for the preservation of its wilderness areas, have inspired a generation of conservationists. The wild area of the State's west and south-west is one of only three large temperate wilderness areas remaining in the southern hemisphere. In 1982 Tasmania's three largest national parks were placed on the World Heritage life by UNESCO in recognition of their outstanding international significance. Additions in 1989 now mean that almost 1.4 million hectares, more than one-fifth of the State, is protected under an international convention so that it will be carefully managed and passed on undiminished to future generations.

Now known as the "World Heritage Area", this vast tract of land is an outstanding example of the earth evolutionary history and is large enough and sufficiently undisturbed, to sustain complete natural systems. Many rare or threatened species survive here, including some which are virtually living fossils.

The Tasmanian wilderness has been opened up to some extent for all kinds of travellers and is no longer just for experienced bushmen. It has many short walks and plenty of opportunities for sightseeing, nature study, bird watching, photography, trout fishing (but get a licence first!), boating, swimming or just relaxing. Scenic flights over the area operate from most major centres in Tasmania. Details are available from Tasmanian Visitor Information Centres.

THE TASMANIAN WILDERNESS

Landscapes

Tasmania's World Heritage Area comprises 1.4 million hectares, about 20 per cent of the State. It stretches from Marakiipa Cave in the north, to Maatsuyker Island in the south, Macquarie Harbour in the west, and South-East Cape in the east. There are more than 1,000 km of walking tracks and about half a million people pay a visit each year. In it is some of Australia's most dramatic landscapes: material for every artist and shutterbug. Untamed rivers, broad lakes and rugged mountains exist almost untouched since their formation before man set foot on Tasmania.

The origin of the central south-west mountains reaches back to between 700 and 1000 million years ago. Sediments deposited at the time were later folded and heated under enormous pressure to form the white quartzite and schist of mountains like Frenchmans Cap and Federation Peak.

In the south-east and north, the remnants of a dolerite plateau cap mountains like Precipitous Bluff and Mount Ossa. The pipe-like structure of dolerite gives these mountains their peculiar block form.

Glaciers and ancient river systems have carved spectacular gorges and formed jagged ridges. The last glaciers peaked about 20,000 years ago. The sea level was lower then and the far south-west contained some broad river estuaries in huge valleys. As the glaciers melted, the sea level rose and the oceans flooded in, drowning the valleys, creating beautiful coastline inlets like Port Davey and Bathurst Harbour.

Plant life

More than 55 million years ago the super-continent of Gondwana broke up to form South America, New Zealand, Australia and Antarctica. Today Tasmania is the Australian stronghold of descendants of the ancient plant life of Gondwana. Unlike the bush on much of the Australian continent, the World Heritage Area contains alpine heath, tall open eucalypt forests and large areas of cool temperate rainforest and moorlands. There are many striking sights for visitors — the autumn gold of the fagus and the red flowers of the waratah against a background of spring and summer snow, or alpine heath looking like a landscaped rockery. Huge gum trees grow in tall open forests on the eastern edge of the high rainfall belt. To the west grow the largest cool temperate rainforests in Australia. The dense canopy of myrtle beech dominated rainforest blocks out the sun, creating a shady world of ferns and mosses. In wet riverine areas grow stands of Huon pine. They are amongst the earth's oldest living things and some are believed to date back before the birth of Christ.

Animal life

Several mammals which were once widespread on the Australian mainland have lived on in Tasmania. These include all of the world's remaining large predatory marsupials. Two-thirds of Tasmania's 33 mammal species are found in the World Heritage Area.

Lesser-known, but equally fascinating animals also live there. One such creature is Tasmania's *freshwater shrimp* which is found only in alpine tarns and streams. It has remained virtually unchanged for over 200 million years. The *orange-bellied parrot* is one of the world's rarest birds, with only about 200 known to exist. It breeds in the south-west and migrates to the Mainland for the winter. The *red-head velvet worm* is only known to exist in one location — a small area in the heart of the South-West National Park. It lives in rotting logs and captures its prey by pinning it down with a fine stream of sticky glue fired from the projections at either side of its head. The *Pedra Branca skink,* isolated since the last Ice Age on a tiny rock island off the south coast, survives on fish scraps dropped by nesting sea birds.

Aboriginal history
People lived in caves and rock shelters in the valleys of south-west Tasmania well before the last Ice Age began 25,000 years ago. Many of these shelters were used throughout the Ice Age. More than 50 caves in the area have been found to contain evidence of human habitation. Painted caves such as Ballawinne and Wargata Mina contain some of the earliest cave paintings in the world. Bands of Aboriginal hunters were the world's most southerly inhabitants during the Ice Age. With the warmer climate which began 13,000 years ago, the open grassy valleys gradually filled with forest, and Aboriginal people moved into the high country formerly covered with a permanent ice cap.

Over the last 3000 years at least four bands of Aborigines occupied the coastal regions of the South-West. They lived in the area for most of the year, moving along a network of well-defined tracks, and hunting and gathering their food from the shoreline and nearby coastal plains. They left large middens as evidence of their age-old occupation of the land.

Park fees
Despite some public indignation, the Parks and Wildlife Service introduced park fees to help maintain Tasmania's parks and

reserves. A range of national park passes lets you choose the most economical way to visit for your needs. Probably the best pass is the two-month holiday pass, at $30 per vehicle — more than enough for your holiday. A daily rate is available at $9 per vehicle or $3 per person.

Passes are available from Tasmanian Visitor Information Centres, park entrances and many tourism-related outlets.

Weather and safety

The weather in the National Heritage Area is very fickle. Sunshine, cloudless skies and 30C heat can be followed by high winds, hail, sleet and snow, even in summer. You should always carry waterproofs, a woollen jumper and hat, map and extra food, even if only planning a half-day walk. The best way to dress is in layers—a singlet or T-shirt first, then a long-sleeved shirt or skivvy, then a jumper, so you can take off or put on another layer as required. If you don't have proper bushwalking gear, long trousers are better than short trousers, even in summer for a short walk. Woollen trousers will be warmer when they are wet.

A few people have died of exposure in the World Heritage Area, so always be prepared. Before you start out leave your plans for the walk with the ranger or your accommodation or a member of your group who isn't going. Remember to contact them when you get back.

Even on a half-day walk you should carry:
- a raincoat or japara
- a warm woollen jumper
- a hat against sun and to keep in warmth
- sunglasses for protection from glare of sun or snow
- worn-in, sturdy walking shoes with woollen socks
- some extra food for instant energy
- a basic first-aid kit
- whistles for children
- a map and compass
- toilet paper and a trowel to bury faecal matter.

Minimal impact bushwalking

This travel guide has not been written for travellers who are planning long treks through the wilderness areas. Overnight stays in the National Heritage Area obviously call for much more planning than walks of only a few hours. However the Parks and Wildlife Service recommends the following measures which should be kept in mind. The vegetation in much of the area is fragile and can be degraded or destroyed by too much walking. Escaped fires have sometimes destroyed wilderness areas for ever.

• Stay on the track even if it is rough or muddy. Walking on the track edges and cutting corners on zigzag tracks increases damage, erosion and visual scarring.

• Spread out in open country where there are no tracks. Spreading out, rather than following in each other's footsteps, disperses the impact on the environment.

• Avoid sensitive vegetation. Sphagnum bogs, cushion plants and other sensitive vegetation are easily destroyed by trampling. Stay on rocks and hard ground when possible.

• Don't cut new tracks or mark tracks with cairns or tape.

• Use only dead fallen wood for fires. Dead standing trees are a home for wildlife. Much of the National Heritage Area is fuel stove only in any case. When in doubt, don't light a fire.

• Don't leave rubbish. If you've carried it in, carry it out.

• Don't wash in streams and lakes. Don't throw food scraps in the water.

HARTZ MOUNTAINS NATIONAL PARK

Only 90 minutes from Hobart, this is the perfect place to experience Tasmania's alpine country and see the effects of ancient glaciers. Sculpted by glaciers and extremes of weather, the 7200 hectares of the park offer spectacular landscapes with both wet eucalypt forest and alpine heath. Because of its easy access from the Huon Valley and relatively short walking distances, this park is one of the best areas in the state for the day visitor. A walk to the 1255 metre-high Hartz Peak will take about 1.5 to 2 hours.

Its wonderful views of the South-West make it worth the modest effort required to hike there.

There are several other signposted walks. One of them is a fully duckboarded walk to Lake Osborne, an ice-carved tarn set against the splendour of the so-called Devil's Backbone. Rain falls on more than 220 days of the year, so you ought to take waterproofs and warm clothing with you at all times. Even in summer, you can encounter rain, snow and mist. But don't be deterred - the clouds of mist shrouding the moors and rocky hills and buffetting winds help you to understand the power of the Tasmanian wilderness. And when the sun breaks through, you can see the wildflowers and the sparkling tarns.

The park can be reached by driving through Geeveston on the Huon Highway, with the last 15 km a gravel track.

For information about weather conditions, ring the regional office on (03) 6298-1577.

SOUTH-WEST NATIONAL PARK

With an area of 608,000ha, this is the largest of Tasmania's national parks. Rugged peaks and thickly-forested valleys are interspersed with extensive buttongrass plains. Most of the park remains completely untouched and bushwalking off well-marked tracks is only for the experienced. It can be approached from south of Hobart, past Dover, or from west of Hobart, past New Norfolk and Mt Field.

Lake Pedder and Strathgordon

From the north, you enter the park from the Lyell Highway. Past Mount Field, the last real town is Maydeena, a dying hamlet where the signs in shop windows are sometimes years old. (It is the last place to buy petrol. None is sold in Strathgordon.) The first attraction is the Junee Cave State Reserve, ten minutes north of Maydeena, off a right-hand turn, as indicated by a sign. There is a platform from which you can see a river spewing from an underground cave system. An informative cassette tape is available from the toll gate near Maydena. At Frodshams Pass a left fork heads south on gravel towards the shores of Lake Pedder. The road eventually reaches the Huon Campground near Scotts Peak Dam. At the lakes there is boating and fishing, with picnic areas and camping grounds.

The Mount Anne circuit, Western Arthurs and Federation Peak are popular, though challenging, walks in this area. Go equipped with rain gear, as in an area with three metres of rain a year, you can expect a shower or two every day. For information about weather conditions, ring the regional office on (03) 6288-1149.

It is hard to describe the wilderness here. Wild and vast, with impassable rainforest, open moors and low scudding cloud, it is a different world to the mellow contours of the Derwent Valley landscape. The knife-edge quartzite hills slicing the sky have names like The Needles, the Sawback Range and Mount Wedge. It looks as though God had run his fingers through wet concrete in the dawn of the world and walked away. It is often cloudy and drizzling, but even in these misty conditions, the crazy silhouettes are extraordinary. Make sure that you take your camera.

The Creepy Crawly Nature Walk, down the Scotts Peak Road, to the left, is an excellent place to experience real rainforest with the comfort of duckboards winding up and down through the bush. Water is always dripping from the dense foliage into the moss blanketing everything. Children will enjoy the interpretive signs which teach them about how a rainforest lives.

Back along the Gordon River Road there are a number of lookouts and picnic spots. The camp grounds at Wedge River below the Sentinel Range and Huon River are ideal for short stops. You can swim in a sandy cove at Teds Beach as well. Before the reaching the Gordon Dam, you pass through Strathgordon, now nearly a ghost town. At its peak, in the 60s and 70s, the township had a population of 2000, with a school of 230 students and a complete range of facilities. Now only a handful of people live there to man the dam. The dam has created Australia's largest water storage, with about 27 times the volume of water in Sydney Harbour. At 140 metres, the Gordon Dam itself is the highest concrete arch structure in the South Hemisphere. You can walk down a steel stairway and across the dam. (Not recommended if you are scared of heights!) There are 45-minute bus tours of the underground power station daily at 10am and 2pm (except Christmas Day and Good Friday) for $5.

The Gordon River Dam complex was one of Australia's most controversial engineering projects which blocks an awesome cleft in the rocks. It flooded Lake Pedder and its famous quartzite beaches and made environmentalists determined to resist further encroachment upon the rugged wilderness. In more recent times there has been an attempt to rally support for pulling the plug on Pedder by releasing water from the Serpentine and Scotts Peak dam. Unfortunately that proposal died after counter-claims from counter-greenies that restoring the lake would destroy what had become possibly the largest platypus habitat in Australia.

Cockle Creek

From the south, the attraction for tourists who want day walks is the four-hour return walk from Cockle Creek to South Cape Bay. To reach it, consult a map and drive as far south from Hobart as you can, past Dover and Southport. Once a nightmarish track through knee-deep mud, the walk is now almost entirely on raised duckboards and allows visitors access to the windswept beaches and headlands of this large bay. After crossing Blowhole Valley and some shady patches of forest, you arrive on an immense cliff ledge looking down on South Cape Bay and the Southern Ocean. Then you can descend a long staircase to a long white beach and admire Lion Rock, a beautiful offshore feature. South from here is the Antarctic and the water is chilly. For information about weather conditions, ring the regional office on (03) 6298-1577.

Melaleuca

If you really want to get away from it all, try flying into Melaleuca, an enclave in the south of the State which is not part of the World Heritage Area. There is a tiny settlement (population: two tin miners), a few rare orange bellied parrots and duckboarded walks through silent wilderness untouched by man. Par Avion organises flights over Port Davey and Bathurst Harbour. You can land at Melaleuca and even camp there. The cost for the "day in the wilderness" package is $240 per person. Contact Par Avion for other deals on (03) 6248-5390.

THE OVERLAND TRACK

The Cradle Mountain Lake St Clair National Park is world-renowned for its dramatic scenery, trackless forests and unspoilt lakes and waterfalls. It is a high country park that takes in Tasmania's tallest mountain, Mount Ossa (1617 metres) and many other smaller but equally spectacular mountains. Cradle Mountain is 1545 metres high.

The most famous track in Tasmania lies between Cradle Mountain and Lake St Clair in the south. For interstate and overseas visitors it offers an exotic contrast to the dusty red outback pictures of the Mainland. The track is 80 km long and with side trips most walkers spend six to eight days on their journey. Most leave between November and Easter and most of them from the Cradle Mountain end. About 4500 people do the walk each year. It is well marked, but often very muddy and rough.

Hiking clubs throughout Australia arrange parties to walk through the National Park to Lake St Clair, along the 85 km Overland Track from Waldheim, and unless you are a very experienced hiker, you should go with one of these parties. For those who haven't the time or the inclination to hike, charter flights are available from Devonport, and you should inquire at the Tourist Office.

Cradle Mountain

Cradle Mountain is one of the best-known features of the Tasmanian wilderness, a great rocky plug rising from level country. Not long ago, a London newspaper ranked it with Italy's Lake Como, Scotland's Loch Lomond and Canada's Niagra Falls.

One of the easy family walks is the three-hour Dove Canyon track, just across from Cradle Mountain Lodge. Less adventurous visitors can take it easy and walk about 2 km along duckboarding to three waterfalls in the middle of the rainforest.

Another 5.5 km further down the road is Waldheim, a small chalet with more information. Perhaps the best walk for families is the two-hour, 6 km circuit of Dove Lake through the Ballroom Forest, passing beneath Cradle Mountain. You'll see the much-photographed boat shed with the mountain in the distance. Along the way are myrtle, pandani plants, heath and massive King Billy pines.

From Waldheim you can also take the Weindorfers forest walk, which takes an easy grade through a forest of King Billy pines, celery-top pines and myrtles. Or drive to Lake Dove and from the car park take a short stroll along either shore until you reach Weindorfers boat shed or Suicide Rock. If the weather is good, there are excellent views of Cradle Mountain. For information about weather conditions, ring the regional office on **(03) 6492-1133.**

HOW TO GET THERE

Approaching the northern entrance: from the Bass Highway, turn south towards the town of Wilmot between Devonport and Ulverstone. Continue south for about 60 km to the park entrance at Cradle Mountain.

Maxwell's operates a charter bus and taxi service from Devonport, Launceston or Hobart to Lake St Clair and Cradle Mountain and from Lake St Clair to Cradle Mountain, (03) 6492-1431 in Wilmot and (03) 6424-8093 in Devonport. TWT Tassielink operates from Cradle Mountain to Devonport and Launceston, and

from Lake St Clair to Devonport, Launceston and Hobart, **(03) 6334-4442** or a Tasmanian Visitor Information Centre.

The Cradle Mountain Visitor Centre (open daily 8am-5pm) has helpful staff, and informative displays and exhibits. Behind the centre is a 15 minute fully-duckboarded forest walk that ends at the roaring Pencil Pine Falls and is suitable even for wheelchairs.

ACCOMMODATION

Daily transport service operates to Lake Dove. Camping is not permitted in Cradle Valley. Contact the Tourist Information Centre in Devonport for further information.

Cradle Mountain Lodge, on the park boundary, **(03) 6492-1303.**
This lodge in the middle of the Tasmanian wilderness has won international acclaim for its unforgettable surroundings, fine food and high standard of accommodation. You can also buy unleaded petrol (an important detail) and basic food supplies. Activities include trail rides, bush walking, fishing and canoeing. Double $174-225.

Cradle Mountain Highlanders, 3876 Cradle Mountain Road **(03) 6492-1116.**
Double B&B $88-160.

Cradle Mountain Campground Tourist Park and Cam Ground, 3832 Cradle Mountain Road (2 km outside the park) **(03) 6492-1395.**
Hostel: double $$32-40 (linen extra). Cabins: double $65-80.

Waldheim Cabins, Cradle Mountain **(03) 6492-1110.**
8 units, double $55-75.

LAKE ST CLAIR

At the southern end is Lake St Clair, Australia's deepest lake (200 metres) and the source of the River Derwent that traverses Hobart. From Cynthia Bay there are at least two top walks that anyone can do. The shorter trek is called the Watersmeet Walk and offers interpretive signs about the lush forest full of tea tree, stringybark and banksia. After about 20 to 30 minutes up the Overland Track, you arrive at the raging confluence of the Hugel and Cuvier Rivers. There is also a pleasant and undemanding three-hour return walk to Shadow and Forgotten Lakes.

Another interesting walk leads past Watersmeet to Platypus Bay. Cross the Watersmeet bridge and take the marked track that follows the Cuvier River to its mouth. Platypus are often seen here

diving for food (mostly by quiet people with lots of patience). In the distance you may sight the outlines of a wrecked barge which was used during the construction of a hydro-electric scheme in 1937. For information about weather conditions, ring the regional office on (03) 6289-1115.

HOW TO GET THERE

If you are driving, follow the Lyell Highway (the A10 to Queenstown) until you meet the Lake St Clair turn-off at Derwent Bridge.

Tasmanian Redline Coaches, of Hobart, operates a Monday to Saturday service from Hobart to Derwent Bridge. Maxwell's operates a charter bus and taxi service from Devonport, Launceston or Hobart to Lake St Clair and Cradle Mountain and from Lake St Clair to Cradle Mountain,

(03) 6492-1431 in Wilmot and (03) 6424-8093 in Devonport. TWT Tassielink operates from Cradle Mountain to Devonport and Launceston, and from Lake St Clair to Devonport, Launceston and Hobart, (03) 6334-4442 or a Tasmanian Visitor Information Centre.

ACCOMMODATION

Lakeside St Clair Wilderness Holidays, Cynthia Bay, **(03) 6289-1137,** 6 cabins, double B&B $160-168.

Derwent Bridge Chalets, Lyell Highway, **(03) 6289-1000,** 4 cabins, double B&B $120.

Derwent Bridge Wilderness Hotel, Lyell Highway, **(03) 6289-1144,** 7 rooms, double B&B $75-85. Chalet double $40.

WALLS OF JERUSALEM

This park is becoming more and more popular. Steep mountains create a natural amphitheatre in a scenic subalpine wilderness. In this high and exposed area, hikers should be prepared for inclement weather. For information about weather conditions, ring the regional office on (03) 6471-7122.

This park covers 51,800 hectares of wilderness and lakes, and is best known for the massive cliffs rising from a landscape dotted with tiny tarns. It is not as easy to get to the Walls as to the main features of other parks in Tasmania. A long, steep two-hour walk from Fish River car park leads to the restored Trappers Hut. Half an hour later you arrive at the park's first delight, a picture-perfect chain of tiny clear lakes called Solomons Jewels. Two hours further on are the Walls themselves. Mount Jerusalem is 1458 metres high. Around a natural basin called The Amphitheatre are groves of 300-year-old pencil pines, an incredibly hardy species that somehow survives the howling sub-zero cold of the highlands winter. Just above Lake Salome, on the edge of the Pool of Siloam, is an especially attractive grove of pencil pines.

.

If you are travelling by car, follow the Bass Highway to Deloraine, then to Mole Creek and Mersey Forest Road.

Maxwell's operates a charter bus and taxi service from Devonport or Launceston to the Walls of Jerusalem, **(03) 6492-1431** in Wilmot and **(03) 6424-8093** in Devonport. TWT Tassielink operates charter buses from Devonport and Launceston **(03) 6334-4442** or a Tasmanian Visitor Information Centre.

Franklin-Gordon Wild Rivers National Park

This 440,000 hectare park forms the central portion of the World Heritage Area. The Franklin River attracts wilderness adventurers from around the world and is considered to be one of the most challenging rafting rivers in Australia. Most people think of this park as the most remote and inaccessible part of the State, but in fact many spectacular views are readily accessible by car. The Lyell Highway passes right through the park from Derwent Bridge to Queenstown.

Along the Lyell Highway

Not far from Derwent Bridge is King William Saddle, a lookout that provides a fine view of the King William Range to the south and Mount Rufus to the north. The saddle is on the main divide between the Derwent River, which flows to the east, and the westward-flowing Gordon-Franklin system. (Don't be surprised if it is raining — it rains 300 days a year in the park.)

From Surprise Valley lookout you may be able to see Frenchmans Cap (1443 metres) in the distance to the south-west. The mountain often retains its snow well into the summer, but even without snow it looks white and shiny because of the quartzite rock in the peak. The unusual formation was thought to resemble a cap worn by Frenchmen.

After a steep descent from Mount Arrowsmith the highway crosses the Franklin River. There is a large parking area with toilets, an information booth and picnic tables. An easy 25-minute return walk through dense rainforest brings you to a riverside platform near the junction of the Franklin and Surprise Rivers. With duckboarded or hardened track all the way, the Franklin River Nature Trail can be managed by people in wheelchairs with a bit of help.

Three kilometres west of the Franklin River bridge begins the walking track to Frenchmans Cap. You can take a 15-minute stroll to the Franklin River and let the experienced walkers pass by on their four to five day return walk to the Cap. The Donaghys Hill Wilderness Lookout is a chance for view of a spectacular wilderness panorama which includes the Franklin River valley and Frenchmans Cap. The walk takes about 40 minutes return on a well-graded track.

The highway crosses the Collingwood River, the departure point for raft or canoe trips down the Franklin River, of which the Collingwood is a tributary. A ten minute walk will take you to the Alma River Crossing.

Just east of **Queenstown,** off the Lyell Highway, is the picturesque Nelsons Falls walk. It winds past creeks through a diverse forest and arrives at a viewing platform overlooking roaring falls. It is a safe and easy track for young and old — wilderness in comfort.

For one of Tasmania's most memorable accessible wilderness walks, try the Kelly Basin Track, deep in the World Heritage Area, which was once a short rail line for hauling ore to waiting boats in Macquarie Harbour. Getting to it is a bit tricky, but can be managed with an ordinary vehicle with good wheel clearance. Drive south from Queenstown down the Mt Jukes and Mt McCall Roads to the Bird River Bridge. (Stop along the way at the Newell Creek rainforest viewing platform.) Watch for a sign on the right for the "Kelly Basin Track". The 90-minute walk begins on your left. You walk along the fast-flowing Bird River through thick rainforest, which gradually gives way to open bracken. The flat, wide track was once a railroad right-of-way. Finally you reach the ruins of Pillinger, a long-abandoned mining town on the shores of Macquarie Harbour, that is now being overgrown by the rainforest.

Mt. Gould, Cradle Mountain/Lake St. Clair National Park

Outlying Islands

KING ISLAND

King Island has become famous throughout Australia for its dairy products and beef — so famous that some bodgey operators are marketing products which never saw the Bass Strait. Locals tell the story of King Island rabbit on the menu of a Sydney restaurant - but rabbits have never been sighted on the island. More than a name on a map, King Island is a synonym for gourmet produce.

King Island is a low plateau, 70 km long and 28 km wide, midway between Victoria and Tasmania at the western end of Bass Strait. It has a population of about 2,800, with two main towns — Currie on the west coast and Grassy in the south-east. Currie is the administrative centre and has almost all the available accommodation. The climate is mild but often rainy, with an annual rainfall of about 1000 mm and only occasional frosts or days over 32C. The terrain ranges from sandy beaches to rain forests with enormous tree ferns and green paddocks, much like Ireland.

The island was first sighted by the English in 1797 and was claimed for the British Crown in 1802 by a Lieutenant Robbins at Sea Elephant Bay. A French ship was sheltering nearby at the same time and the English had to borrow dry powder from them for the salute.

Opposite: Hop fields in the Derwent Valley

Gangs of sealers soon invaded the island and slaughtered the seals and sea elephants so indiscriminately that they are only occasionally sighted to this day. Hunters followed, spending months on the island in pursuit of kangaroos, whose skins they would sell in Victoria or Tasmania.

During the Nineteenth Century there were some appalling shipwrecks and remarkable survivals, especially on the west Coast. Australia's worst marine disaster occurred in 1845 when the *Cataraqui,* a ship full of immigrants, ran ashore on the west coast and 399 people were lost. There is a small monument commemorating the tragedy. Occasionally bits of the ship are still washed ashore.

The continuing shipwrecks prompted the Victorian Government to build a companion lighthouse at Cape Otway. The King Island lighthouse, a massive granite building, was built at Cape Wickham on the island's northern tip. But the wrecks continued — in 1866 the keepers had to feed 500 survivors from the wreck of the *Netherby.* After four large ships broke up in a space of ten years, a lighthouse was built at Currie on the east coast. Divers can visit many of the wrecks off shore. Farming remains the most stable industry on the island, although scheelite, the ore for tungsten, gold, tin, lead, slate and rutile have all been mined over the years. Other industries include kelp harvesting and fishing. King Island abounds with wallaby, pheasant, quail, wild turkey and peacocks. The pheasant shooting season is in June; the duck shooting season in March and April; and mutton-birding takes place in the autumn. It is not difficult to see penguins and seals.

HOW TO GET THERE

There are daily flights from Wynyard, Devonport and Moorabbin (Melbourne). Check with your travel agent for details. Car hire
Once you have landed, you may want to rent a car. Remember that RACT breakdown service is not available. Howell's Auto Rent, Meech Street, Currie, **(03) 6462-1282.** Cheapa Island Car Rental, Currie, (03) 6462-1603

ACCOMMODATION

King Island is a popular tourist destination and there is a lot of accommodation available, although it is wise to book ahead. Here is a selection, with prices for a double room per night, which should be used as only a guide especially as rates may vary in holidays seasons.

Parer's King Island Hotel, Main Street, Currie, **(03) 6462-1633,** 12 ensuites, double B&B $70-95.

Boomerang by the Sea, Golf Club Road, Currie, **(03) 6462-1288,** 16 ensuites, double B&B $90-102.

King Island Gem Motel, 95 North Road, Currie, **(03) 6462-1260,** 10 ensuites, double B&B $90-100.

Naracoopa Holiday Units, Beach Road, Currie, **(03) 6461-1326,** 2 ensuites, double $80.

Bass Caravan Park, North Road, Currie, **(03) 6462-1260,** 6 caravans, double $45-85.

SIGHTSEEING

Currie Lighthouse

A cast iron lighthouse, it was built in England in 1880, dismantled and shipped to the Island in 312 pieces. This is now a National Trust building, and is open Sat-Sun 2-4pm. Next to the iron lighthouse is the lighthouse keeper's brick cottage, an elegant 1879 building which is now a museum portraying the history of King Island and the native wildlife.

Kelp Industries

This is an interesting King Island industry — kelp is gathered, kiln dried, crushed, and shipped to Scotland, where it is used to manufacture alginate in products as varied as ice cream, hand cream, paint and toothpaste.

Calcified Forest

Tree trunks which were covered by sand 7000 years ago now look like an eerie lunar landscape. Access is off the south road along a sandy track. Cars can be driven to within a few hundred metres of the forest, but the final stage must be done on foot.

Cape Wickham Lighthouse

At 52 metres this is the tallest lighthouse in Australia. Its light can be seen for 54 kilometres. Nearby are a number of graves of men and women drowned off the coast. A bicentennial memorial to the lighthouse keepers was erected in 1988. It is not open to the public but can be viewed from a distance.

FLINDERS ISLAND

Flinders Island is the largest of a collection of the 70 islands in the Furneaux group, a scattered chain of islands in the Bass Strait between Victoria's Wilson's Promontory and Tasmania's Cape Portland. Flinders has a pleasant maritime climate without extremes of temperature, making it a year-round holiday destination. About 1100 people live on the island.

Flinders Island has many deserted beaches and secluded coves with good fishing, mountains and nature reserves. Commercial facilities, including hotel accommodation, shops and petrol are generally only available in the townships of Whitemark and Lady Barron, at the southern end of the island. Those who wish to visit the off-shore islands and wildlife reserves should inquire about charter boat services in Lady Barron. The islands were discovered by Tobias Furneaux, the captain of James Cook's support ship, *Adventure,* in 1773, and later charted by Matthew Flinders. In the late eighteenth century the seal-hunting colony established on Cape Barren Island, the island immediately south of Flinders

Island, became the first white settlement south of Sydney. The sealers kidnapped Aboriginal women and the descendants of these unions are numbered amongst today's Tasmanian Aborigines, some of whom still live in the Furneaux Group. These "Straitsmen" were joined in 1831 by the remnants of the Aboriginal tribes of Tasmania. At the settlement of Wybalenna they were to be educated and trained as 'useful' Christian workers. Their chapel, now the only building associated with the first Tasmanians, is an important historical monument.

HOW TO GET THERE

There are about three flights a day from Launceston, Hobart via Launceston and Taralgon, in Victoria. Consult your travel agent for details.

Car hire

Once you land on Flinders Island, you will want to rent a car. Remember that RACT breakdown service is not available. Flinders Island Car Rentals, Whitemark, **(03) 6359-2168** Bowman Lees Car Hire, Whitemark, **(03) 6359-2014** Flinders Island Transport Services, Whitemark, **(03) 6359-2060** Furneaux Car Rental, **(03) 6359-2112**

ACCOMMODATION

Flinders Island is a popular tourist destination and there is a lot of accommodation available, although it is wise to book ahead. Here is a selection, with prices for a double room per night, which should be used as only a guide especially as rates may vary in holidays seasons.

Interstate Hotel, Whitemark, **(03) 6359-2114,**
9 ensuites, double B&B $75.

Yaringa Holiday Cottages, Holloway Street, Lady Barron,
(03) 6359-4522;
3 ensuites, double $70.

Flinders Island Lodge, Lady Barron, **(03) 6359-3521,**
13 ensuites, double B&B $96-168.

SIGHTSEEING

Wybalenna Chapel
This is the site of the doomed attempt to remove the remaining
Aborigines from Tasmania. Today all the buildings are in ruins,
except for the Chapel, which has been restored by the National
Trust. Wybalenna is of great significance to today's Tasmanian
Aboriginal people.

Furneaux Lookout
On Summer Camp Road, this is a bicentennial memorial to Tobias
Furneaux.

Strzelecki National Park
Flinders Island's only national park features a mountain rising to
756 metres which offers panoramic views - on a clear day, as far as
Tasmania and Victoria. The 4215 hectare park is named after the
Polish explorer Count Paul Edmund Strzelecki, who climbed its
peaks in 1842. There is a well-marked three-kilometre walking
track to the summit of the Strzelecki Peaks. Another highlight,
Trousers Point, is an ideal camping spot with enticing swimming
beaches.

Emita Museum
This museum illustrates the sad history of the early Aboriginal
settlement as well as natural and maritime history. Open Sat-Sun
2-5pm, and daily 2-5pm during school holidays.

Patriarch Wildlife Sanctuary
A small, privately owned conservation area on the east coast, with rugged granite hills, beaches, swamps, lagoons and a beautiful estuary. It is an official bird banding station and has some accommodation for study groups, 003-59-2024.

Logan Lagoon Wildlife Sanctuary
This is a wonderful wetland where an abundance of birdlife can be found, although water levels drop in summer. It is a refuge site for the Cape Barren goose and has been included in the List of Wetlands of International Importance.

Mount Killiecrankie
Flinders Island is widely known as a source of topaz (locally called Killiecrankie diamonds), and smoky and crystal quartz. Tourists can fossick for the gemstones in Mines Creek or Diamond Gully on the southern side of Mount Killiecrankie.

MACQUARIE ISLAND
From Macquarie Island to the Antarctic is only about three days sailing if the weather is right. Believe it or not, this isolated chunk of rock is a small part of Tasmania 1466 km south-east of Hobart which is home to about 20 scientists, 100,000 seals and four million penguins. It is the best preserved fragment of deep ocean crust known above sea level and in 1997 it was declared a World Heritage site. The island is 34 km long and up to 5 km wide. It is mainly a long plateau ranging from 100 to 350 metres above sea level that is bounded on all sides by steep slopes or cliffs. There are several larger lakes and many smaller lakes and tarns. Opinions have varied on its appeal. The weather is awful: cold, wet, windy and foggy. The average daily temperature is 3.5C. Even in the early days of the colony, it was agreed that this remote and stormy island was unfit even for a penal colony. There are no trees, just tussock grass and Macquarie Island cabbage. In 1822 a sea captain commented that it was "the most wretched place of involuntary

and slavish exilium that can possibly be conceived". Nowadays it is regarded as one of the richest wildlife sanctuaries in the world. As the only land in millions of square kilometres of ocean, it is a breeding ground for millions of birds, including albatrosses, petrels and skuas and four species of penguins. Until early this century, the island was exploited by sealers who hunted the Macquarie Island fur seal almost to extinction, and then began to work on other species. Fortunately several scientists, particularly Sir Douglas Mawson, the Antarctic explorer, lobbied to have it declared a nature reserve, which it is today. The depredation of the sealers are now only memories, with their try pots and camp sites scattered over the shore.

Macquarie Island can only be reached by sea. It is the most remote, most difficult and most expensive place in Tasmania to visit, but it is like no other place on earth, with its heavy cloud cover, gusting westerly winds, skies teeming with birds, and the bellowing of massive elephant seals. At the moment, the island is closed to tourists because too many people took up the option when tours were organised. Alas! Anyhow, even when tourists anchored offshore, there was no guarantee that they would be able to land in the heavy seas. Eight vessels are known to have been wrecked there, one as late as 1988: the Nella Dan, a resupply vessel for the scientists working there.

TASSIE TRIVIA

In 1893, Hobart became the first city in the Southern Hemisphere to run an all-electric tram system and the first with double-deckers making regular runs.

Errol Flynn, swashbuckling hero of many Hollywood films, was born in Hobart in 1909.

The Bush Inn at New Norfolk (1825) is the oldest continually licensed pub in Australia.

The Theatre Royal in Hobart is Australia's oldest continuously operating live theatre.

Tasmania has a higher proportion of its land area reserved for recreation and conservation purposes than any other state: 22.6%.

Tasmania has the deepest freshwater lake in Australia: Lake St Clair at about 200 metres.

The Cataract Gorge Chairlift in Launceston is the longest single-span chairlift in the world.

Australia's oldest school is Launceston Church Grammar which was founded in 1846 when Launceston was a town of only 8,000.

Tasmania has the largest lavender farm in the world and it is the only commercial lavender producer in the southern hemisphere.

A Huon Pine in the South-West wilderness is estimated to be 10,000 years old, making it the oldest living thing on earth.

Tasmania has 68 golf courses — more per capita than any other state in Australia.

Tasmania has Australia's oldest golf course. The first golf was played in Australia in the Midlands town of Bothwell in 1839.

The Van Diemen's Land Company, which has operated Woolnorth since 1825, is the only royal charter company in the world which is still trading.

Atlantic salmon grow faster in Tasmanian waters than anywhere else in the world.

The first telephone call in Australia was made in Tasmania, connecting Launceston with Campbell Town in the Midlands.

Launceston had the first electric lighting system in the Southern Hemisphere.

Cape Barren Island, the island immediately south of Flinders Island, became the first white settlement south of Sydney in the late eighteenth century when sealers camped there.

Tasmania's southernmost point is Macquarie Island, 1,466 km south-east of Hobart and 1,294 km from Antarctica.

The highest mountain in Tasmania is Mount Ossa, at 1,617m. The longest river is the South Esk, at 201 km.

Australia's oldest synagogue is on Argyle Street in Hobart. It is the only one in the world with seats set aside for convicts to worship.

Hobart is one of the few places in the world where you can play the ancient game of Royal Tennis and it has the only original court in Australia.

The Cascade Brewery in South Hobart, established in 1832, is Australia's oldest brewery.

The beautiful stone Richmond Bridge over the Coal River, built in 1823, is the oldest still in use in Australia.

Oatlands, in Tasmania's Midlands, has the largest number of Georgian sandstone buildings in a village in Australia.

The only Australian to have been both a State Premier and Prime Minister of the Commonwealth was a Tasmanian, Joseph Lyons.

The Gordon River Power Development is Australia's largest water storage, with about 27 times the volume of water in Sydney Harbour.

At 140 metres, the Gordon Dam is the highest concrete arch structure in the South Hemisphere.

The enlarged Lake Pedder is thought to have become the largest platypus habitat in the world.

Experience the difference! In Alonnah you can drink at the Hotel Bruny, "Australia's most southern hotel". In Dover you can drink at the Dover Hotel, "Australia's southernmost Hotel Motel". In Southport you can drink at the Southport Settlement, "Australia's most southern watering hole". Take your pick.

INDEX

The old Lunatic Asylum – now a gift shop

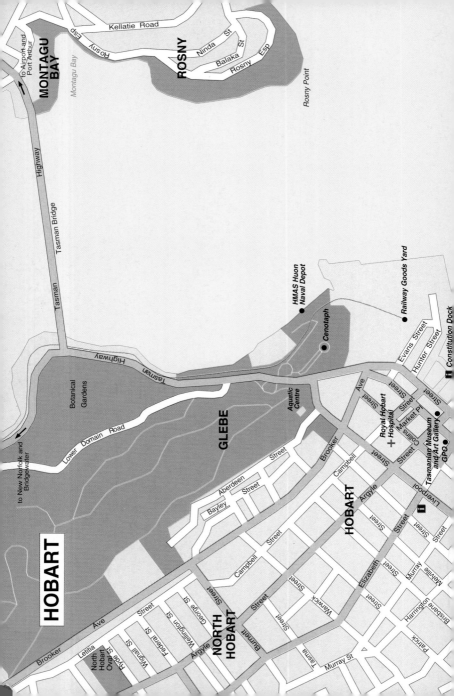